Animated Movies

FACTS, FIGURES & FUN

"Any book without a mistake in it has had
too much money spent on it"

Sir William Collins, publisher

Animated Movies

FACTS, FIGURES & FUN

JOHN
GRANT

ff&f

For Lynn and Kate Perkins

Animated Movies
Facts, Figures & Fun

Published by
Facts, Figures & Fun, an imprint of
AAPPL Artists' and Photographers' Press Ltd.
Church Farm House, Wisley, Surrey GU23 6QL
info@ffnf.co.uk www.ffnf.co.uk
info@aappl.com www.aappl.com

Sales and Distribution
UK and export: Turnaround Publisher Services Ltd.
orders@turnaround-uk.com
USA and Canada: Sterling Publishing Inc.
sales@sterlingpub.com
Australia & New Zealand: Peribo Pty.
peribomec@bigpond.com
South Africa: Trinity Books. trinity@iafrica.com

A catalogue record for this book is available from the
British Library.

ISBN 13: 9781904332527
ISBN 10: 1904332528

Design (contents and cover): Malcolm Couch
mal.couch@blueyonder.co.uk

Printed in China by Imago Publishing
info@imago.co.uk

CONTENTS

It Lives! (Sort of ...) The Story of Animation

Animated movies – indeed, movies in general – depend upon a phenomenon called the persistence of vision. In brief, our brains, *via* our eyes, do not observe the world in continuous motion, although we think that's the case. Each "picture" of the world that we see has a small but finite duration before it is replaced by the next one. That duration is about 1/18th of a second. The brain smooths together the rapidly succeeding pictures to give the illusion of continuity. This process is replicated in the cinema by projecting images, each differing in detail from the preceding one, at a speed of (typically) 24 per second. The brain interprets this display as a smooth continuity.

The very earliest forms of animation predate the invention of the cinema by thousands of years. Not long after the discovery of the prehistoric cave paintings at Altamira, Lascaux and other sites it was observed that, when viewed by flickering light – such as that from a fire – the images appeared to have an illusory life. Whether this effect came about by deliberate intent of the artists is something we shall never know.

Much closer to our own time came the anonymous invention of the flipbook. As every schoolchild has discovered, if you draw a succession of pictures on the page-corners of a book, then riffle the pages, you create a primitive form of animation. In due course, people began printing illustrated books whose pages could be flipped to show "moving pictures".

The magic lantern was another important early invention. In 1645, Athanasius Kircher, a Jesuit scholar and inventor, published *Ars Magna Lucis et Umbrae* ("The Great Art of Light and Shadow"). His last chapter showed a diagram of the simplest form of magic lantern. Later he refined this, so that painted images on a revolving glass disc could be projected. By the 18th century, entrepreneurs were staging elaborate magic-lantern displays.

A further early invention was the zoetrope. Viewers could look through slits in a revolving drum to see pictures on the drum's opposite interior wall, thereby once more gaining an illusion of motion.

In 1889 the French inventor Emile Reynaud patented his Théatre Optique, which depended upon a device he'd invented, the praxinoscope. First put on public display in 1892, this was a development of the zoetrope capable of projecting images. He was able to present animated "movies" up to about ten minutes long. In 1893 Thomas Edison invented the kinetoscope, a device that allowed a single person to look through a viewer and see successive images on a celluloid film strip. The following year he copyrighted what he claimed as the world's first motion picture, *The Record of a Sneeze*. In 1894 Louis Lumière invented the cinematograph, thereby truly heralding the modern era of the movies. This device could project moving pictures, in the modern sense of the term, onto a screen. And in 1895 the Lumière brothers publicly projected their movie *Workers Leaving the Lumière Factory in Lyons-Montplaisir*. The cinema was born, and the stage was set for animation.

There's great debate about which was the first animated movie, depending upon how tightly one defines "animated movie", but the honour is usually given to *Humorous Phases of Funny Faces* (1906), made by James Stuart Blackton. Not satisfied with having made a 2D-animation movie, Blackton went on in 1907 to create *The Haunted Hotel*, in which, using effects and the technique of stop-motion, he gave 3D animation to the world.

> **STOP-MOTION ANIMATION**
> A form of animation in which, rather than a succession of drawings being used, objects are photographed, then moved slightly, then photographed again, and so on. A variant is clay animation, in which the objects or figures, modelled in clay, are slightly remoulded between each photograph.

In 1908 Emile Cohl, a comic-strip artist, put his professional expertise together with the relatively new techniques of motion pictures to create another candidate for first animated movie: *Fantasmagorie*. It was four minutes long. Where Blackton and others had related their animations to the real world – essentially, they'd used animation as an effect – *Fantasmagorie* was an entirely animated movie. In 1909 Cohl made the live-action/animated *Clair de Lune Espagnol* ("Spanish Moonlight").

Winsor McCay, the "Father of Animation", made his first movie, *Little Nemo*, in 1911. A prolific comic-strip artist noted for the lightning speed with which he drew, he'd taken to presenting a vaudeville act based on this ability. The movie was made as an embellishment for his act, as was his *Gertie the Dinosaur* (1914), a few years later. However, *Gertie* was something more: the drawn dinosaur had a perceived personality, so the movie had more than mere curio value and was shown as a standalone entity in cinemas.

In 1913 John Randolph Bray made the animated short *The Artist's Dreams*. Bray's great breakthrough was the realization that, while the moving figures had to be redrawn repeatedly, the environment in which they moved did not: a single background drawing could be done for an extended period of action. His technique, patented in 1914, was not the best at effecting this; Earl Hurd patented a better one at about the same time. Hurd's technique, cel animation, is still in use today. Bray persuaded Hurd to combine their patents, and the first animation studio was born, initiating the long series of Colonel Heeza Liar animated shorts.

CEL ANIMATION

The principle of cel animation is that the action elements of an animated movie are drawn on a sheet of transparent celluloid (hence "cel"). The sheets are then placed in succession over a still background painting, and the assembly is shot frame by frame. Soon animators were using multiple cels, with different action going on in each of several layers of celluloid.

As celluloid was expensive, a new job came into existence: cel-washer. Once a drawn cel had been photographed, it was the task of the cel-washer to clean it off so that the sheet could be drawn on again.

Also in 1914, the Canadian animator Raoul Barré introduced the peg system. Earlier animators had difficulty keeping the figures they animated in one place – from frame to frame, the character would jerk up and down a little with relation to the background, or from side to side. In Barré's system, the sheets of drawing paper animators used were perforated with holes down each side, and these went over fixed pegs. Similarly, pegs were used when photographing the drawings.

WWI gave the US movie industry a tremendous boost (as would WWII later), because its European rivals were reduced to a shadow of their former selves during hostilities. Further, once the US joined in, there was state-funded moviemaking work galore on offer for propaganda and related purposes. The time-consuming process of animation benefited particularly from the relative tran-

ROTOSCOPING

In 1915 Max Fleischer patented the rotoscope. In this system, the movie would first be shot in live action, then projected frame by frame from under the animator's paper. The animator thus could simply trace the key elements of the action. Rotoscoping is still used fairly extensively in traditional animation today, although it can give a rather lifeless demeanour to the resulting movie.

quility of working in the US. It is only relatively recently that any foreign – i.e., Japanese – animation has come to challenge this US domination.

In 1920 the Bray studio created the first animated movie in full colour – that is, using colour film. (Earlier coloured animations had relied on hand-tinting of the film.) The result was judged too expensive for any increased audience appeal it might have, and the practice was abandoned.

The Lost World (1925), a live-action movie based on the Conan Doyle tale, featured stop-motion animation of the monsters by Willis O'Brien. There were many imitators over the succeeding decades, not least of which was *King Kong* (1933), again featuring O'Brien's handiwork.

The first animated feature movie appeared in 1926: Lotte Reiniger's silent masterpiece *The Adventures of Prince Achmed*, done using mainly her paper-cutout-silhouette technique. Reiniger created a second animated feature, *Dr. Dolittle and his Animals* (1928), but then fates conspired to ensure she never made another.

Walt Disney and Ub Iwerks created their character Mickey Mouse in 1928. They made two Mickey Mouse shorts and were midway through the third, *Steamboat Willie* (1928), when the talkies became all the rage. Swiftly they added a primitive soundtrack, and henceforward the silent animated short was dead. (This was not the first sound animated short, which may have been Paul Terry's *Dinner Time*, a few months earlier, but it was probably the first with an – approximately – synchronized soundtrack.)

Betty Boop and Pluto were "born" in 1930, Goofy in 1932, Popeye (so far as animation is concerned – he came from a comic strip) in 1933, Donald Duck in 1934, Porky Pig in 1935, Daffy Duck, Daisy Duck and Elmer Fudd in 1937, Bugs Bunny in 1938 (although a purist might claim his real debut was in 1940's *A Wild Hare*), Tom &

Jerry and Woody Woodpecker in 1940, Mighty Mouse and Tweety in 1942, Casper, Pepe Le Pew and Sylvester in 1945, Foghorn Leghorn and Heckle & Jeckle in 1946, Marvin Martian and Yosemite Sam in 1948, Mr. Magoo and Roadrunner & Coyote in 1949, Speedy Gonzales in 1953, the Pink Panther in 1964, and Wallace & Gromit in 1989.

The sparsity after 1953 of new series characters for theatrical animated shorts reflects the virtually wholesale evacuation of this style to TV. The first animated series for TV was *Crusader Rabbit*, begun in 1949.

In 1937 Disney released the first animated feature movie in colour; also the first sound animated feature, *Snow White and the Seven Dwarfs* (see page 42). It was followed in 1939 by the Fleischers' first, *Gulliver's Travels* (see page 75).

After the US entered WWII, and even slightly before, the animation studios cranked up their anti-Axis propaganda efforts. Disney's *Der Fuehrer's Face* (1942), in which Donald Duck takes on Hitler, won the 1942 Oscar. Most significant of all these efforts was arguably the Private Snafu series of 26 shorts done for military audiences by Warners, starting with *Coming Snafu* (1943).

In the US the Democrats commissioned in 1944 an independent short animated movie, *Hell Bent for Election*. It was apparently very successful – so much so that (at least according to urban legend) the two parties agreed never again to use the powerful weapon of animation against each other. From then on it was all just the usual good clean stuff – smears, lies, defamations, entrapment …

Disney stopped making Mickey Mouse shorts in 1953, the last being *The Simple Things*. Thereafter the Mouse continued his career exclusively on TV and/or in comics until returning to cinemas in the featurette *Mickey's Christmas Carol* (1983). Disney stopped releasing animated shorts as a matter of policy altogether in 1956, although for special reasons a few have appeared sporadically since.

In 1956 the first major international animation festival appeared as an annexe of the Cannes Film Festival. In 1960 it became an independent festival, held annually at Annecy, France. The following year saw the inauguration in France of ASIFA (Association Internationale de Film d'Animation).

A pioneer computer-animated movie, *Cibernetic 5,3*, made by John Stehura, was presented at the UCLA Animation Workshop in 1967. Thereafter computer animation gradually crept into all aspects of the genre (often going unnoticed amid traditional cel animation). Disney's *TRON* (1982) was the first feature to foreground its computer animation, all 15 minutes of it. Finally Pixar made the breakthrough in 1995 with the first all-CGI feature movie, *Toy Story*. The studio had earlier made some CGI shorts, notably *Tin Toy* (1989), the first CGI movie to win an Oscar.

Ralph Bakshi's *Fritz the Cat* became the first animated feature movie to receive an X-rating in the US on its release in 1972. That year also saw the release of the first Australian animated feature, *Marco Polo Jr. vs. The Red Dragon*, dir Eric Porter.

In 1989 Robert Zemeckis's feature movie *Who Framed Roger Rabbit*, with anim dir Richard Williams, was released, its enormous commercial success heralding a new dawn for the live-action/animated mode – and, indeed, for animated feature movies in general, which had been somewhat in the doldrums. The second whammy of the double whammy was delivered in 1995 by Pixar with *Toy Story*. Or perhaps *Toy Story* was really the third whammy: 1989 also saw the release of Aardman Animations' Oscar-winning *A Grand Day Out*, dir Nick Park. Or even the fourth, because Hayao Miyazaki's *Nausicaä of the Valley of the Wind* (1984) and Katsuhiro Otomo's *Akira* (1987) had between them made the Western cinema-going public emphatically aware of Japanese anime ... Since then animation has become one of the most commercially important genres in cinema, with a high proportion of any year's box-office blockbusters being animated features.

In 2002, bowing at long last to industry pressure, the Academy of Motion Picture Arts and Science introduced a new category for Feature Length Animation. There were nine eligible movies: *Final Fantasy: The Spirits Within*, *Jimmy Neutron: Boy Genius*, *Monsters, Inc.*, *Osmosis Jones*, *The Prince of Light*, *Return to Xanadu*, *Shrek*, *The Trumpet of the Swan* and *Waking Life*. The winner was *Shrek*. The following year, welcome recognition was given to a non-US animator when Hayao Miyazaki's *Spirited Away* took the statue.

"Boop-Oop-a-Doop!"
Betty Boop

"What happened to the kaboom?
There's supposed to be an earthshattering kaboom!"
Marvin Martian

"Th-th-th-that's all, folks!"
Porky Pig

A CHEATLIST OF MASTER ANIMATORS

Animated movies are usually collective efforts, with animated features in particular often commanding huge staffs. But this does not mean the movies are anonymous, or created by committee. Here are a few of the master animators who have shaped the genre, with selected examples of their work.

TEX AVERY

Born: Taylor, Texas, 1908
Notes: The legendary animator who did more than anyone else to shake off the idea that animated "reality" should obey the same rules as the mundane world.
Shorts: *Gold Diggers of '49* (1936), *Cinderella Meets Fella* (1938), *Daffy Duck and Egghead* (1938), *Dangerous Dan McPhoo* (1939), *Thugs With Dirty Mugs* (1939), *Cross Country Detours* (1940), *A Wild Hare* (1940), *Blitz Wolf* (1942), *Dumb Hounded* (1943), *Red Hot Riding Hood* (1943), *Happy-Go-Nutty* (1944), *Swing Shift Cinderella* (1945), *Northwest Hounded Police* (1946), *Little Tinker* (1948), *House of Tomorrow* (1949).
Died: 1980

RALPH BAKSHI

Born: Brooklyn, 1938
Notes: The moviemaker who returned US commercial animation to its role as a medium for adults, not just children.
TV: *The Mighty Heroes* (1966–7), *Spider-Man* (1967–70), *Mighty Mouse: The New Adventures* (1987–9), *Tattertown: A Christmas Special* (1988), *Dr. Seuss' The Butter Battle Book* (1989).
Features: *Fritz the Cat* (1972), *Heavy Traffic* (1973), *Coonskin* (1974;

vt *Streetfight*), *Wizards* (1977), *The Lord of the Rings* (1978), *American Pop* (1981), *Hey Good Lookin'* (1982), *Fire & Ice* (1983), *Cool World* (1992).

RAOUL BARRÉ

Born: Montreal, 1874
Notes: An innovator who founded the world's first commercial animation studio (1914) and invented the peg system (see page 10).
Shorts: *The Animated Grouch Chaser* (1915), *The Hicks in Nightmareland* (1915), *Cooks vs Cooks: The Phable of Olaf and Louis* (1916), *Cramps* (1916), *Feet is Feet: A Phable* (1916), *The Phable of a Busted Romance* (1916).
Died: 1969

BRAD BIRD

Born: Kalispell, Montana, 1957
Notes: Caught the eye of Disney in his early teens, being mentored by Milt Kahl. Later worked there a while, then at Klasky–Csupo helping develop the TV series *The Simpsons* (1989–current). Co-wrote the screenplay for the live-action movie **batteries not included* (1987). After working on TV series like *The King of the Hill* (1997–current) he moved into theatrical animation.
Features: *The Iron Giant* (1999), *The Incredibles* (2004).

DON BLUTH

Born: El Paso, Texas, 1937
Notes: The animator who (with John Pomeroy, Gary Goldman and others) departed Disney in the late 1970s to set up animating in direct competition with Disney, whom they felt had lowered standards for the sake of expediency. Bluth's career since has been one of constant ups and downs, but in the ups he has created a major body of first-rate work.
Shorts: *The Small One* (1978), *Banjo the Woodpile Cat* (1979).
Features: *Pete's Dragon* (1977), *The Secret of NIMH* (1982), *An American Tail* (1986), *The Land Before Time* (1988), *All Dogs Go to Heaven* (1989), *Anastasia* (1997), *Bartok the Magnificent* (1999), *Titan A.E.* (2000).

BRUNO BOZZETTO

Born: Milan, 1938

Notes: Like Ralph Bakshi in the US but with far greater quirkiness and charm, this Italian animator has played a leading role in re-establishing animation as an artform for not just children but adults.

Shorts: *Tapum! La Storia delle Armi* (1958), *An Award for Mister Rossi* (1960), *Mister Rossi Buys a Car* (1966), *A Life in a Tin* (1967), *Ego* (1969), *Pickles* (1971), *Self Service* (1974), *Baby Story* (1978), *Baeus* (1987), *Mister Tao* (1988), *Grasshoppers* (1990), *Drop* (1993), *Point of View* (1998).

TV: *Gli Sport del Signor Rossi* (1975), *Lilliput-put* (1980).

Features: *West and Soda* (1965), *Vip, Mio Fratello Superuomo* (1968), *Allegro non Troppo* (1976), *Mr Rossi Looks for Happiness* (1976), *Mr Rossi's Dreams* (1977), *Le Vacanze del Sig. Rossi* (1977).

BOB CLAMPETT

Born: San Diego, California, 1913

Notes: One of the great animators in the Golden Age of Warners' animated shorts, Clampett went on to have a second major career puppeting and animating for TV.

Shorts: *Porky's Bedtime Story* (1937), *Wabbit Twouble* (1941), *Bugs Bunny Gets the Boid* (1942), *The Hep Cat* (1942), *A Tale of Two Kitties* (1942), *Horton Hatches the Egg* (1942), *Coal Black and de Sebben Dwarfs* (1943), *A Corny Concerto* (1943), *Russian Rhapsody* (1944), *The Great Piggy Bank Robbery* (1946), *Kitty Kornered* (1946), *The Big Snooze* (1946).

TV: *Time for Beany* (1949–54; puppetry), *Beany and Cecil* (1962–88).

Died: 1984

WALT DISNEY

Born: Chicago, 1901

Notes: A hugely influential producer of animated movies, he realized early his own shortcomings as an animator and gave that task to others.

Shorts: *The Four Musicians of Bremen* (1922), *Alice's Wonderland* (1923, released 1928).

TV: Presented numerous Disney broadcasts.

Died: 1966

DAVE FLEISCHER

Born: New York, 1894

Notes: The creative genius behind the Fleischer brothers' long string of animation successes. Initially an assistant to much older brother Max, he relatively soon took over animation, story and other creative aspects. (It's impossible to work out who did what during the transitional period, so some movies credited to Max may be Dave's, and vice versa.)

Shorts: *My Old Kentucky Home* (1926), *Koko Needles the Boss* (1927), *KoKo's Earth Control* (1927), *Noah's Lark* (1929), *Dizzy Dishes* (1930), *Bimbo's Initiation* (1931), *Silly Scandals* (1931), *Boop-Oop-a-Doop* (1932), *Popeye the Sailor* (1933), *Snow-White* (1933), *Poor Cinderella* (1934), *She Reminds Me of You* (1934), *Dancing on the Moon* (1935), *Be Human* (1936), *Popeye the Sailor Meets Sindbad the Sailor* (1936), *Popeye the Sailor Meets Ali Baba's Forty Thieves* (1937), *Aladdin and his Wonderful Lamp* (1939, vt *Popeye Meets Aladdin*), *Yip, Yip, Yippy* (1939), *King for a Day* (1940), *Way Back when the Triangle Had its Points* (1940), *Raggedy Ann and Raggedy Andy* (1941), *Superman* (1941), *Amoozin but Confoozin* (1944).

Features: *Gulliver's Travels* (1939), *Hoppity Goes to Town* (1941).

Died: 1979

MAX FLEISCHER

Born: Vienna, 1883

Notes: The inventive genius behind the Fleischer brothers' long string of animation successes and innovations, latterly largely abandoning creative work in favour of handling the business. He is credited with inventing the rotoscope (although there had been earlier forms).

Shorts: *Out of the Inkwell* (1916), *Experiment No. 1* (1918), *The Tantalizing Fly* (1919), *Modeling* (1921), *My Bonnie (Lies Over the Ocean)* (1925), *Rudolph the Red-Nosed Reindeer* (1944).

Feature: *The Einstein Theory of Relativity* (1923).

Died: 1972

FRIZ FRELENG

Born: Kansas City, Missouri, 1904 (not 1906, as often stated), as Isadore Freleng

Notes: The longest-serving Warners animator of them all, and the one who came away with the most Oscars, thereafter continuing to win awards – and public acclaim – with the DePatie–Freleng Pink Panther animations.

Shorts: *Ain't Nature Grand* (1930), *I Haven't Got a Hat* (1935), *Rhapsody in Rivets* (1941), *Daffy – The Commando* (1943), *Pigs in a Polka* (1943), *Hare Trigger* (1945), *Life With Feathers* (1945), *Tweetie Pie* (1947), *Back Alley Oproar* (1948), *Speedy Gonzales* (1955), *Birds Anonymous* (1957), *Knighty Knight Bugs* (1958), *The Pink Phink* (1964), *Shocking Pink* (1965).

TV: *The Pink Panther Show* (1969–79, vt *The New Pink Panther Show*, vt *The Pink Panther Laugh and a Half Hour and a Half Show*), *The All New Pink Panther Show* (1978–9), *Bugs Bunny's Loony Christmas Tales* (1979).

Features: *Friz Freleng's Looney Looney Looney Bugs Bunny Movie* (1981), *Daffy Duck's Movie: Fantastic Island* (1983), *Bugs Bunny's 3rd Movie: 1001 Rabbit Tales* (1982).

Died: 1995

JOHN HALAS & JOY BATCHELOR

Born (Halas): Budapest, 1912, as Janos Halász
Born (Batchelor): Watford, Hertfordshire, 1914
Notes: For many years the premier UK commercial animators, their studio often described as "the British Disney", Halas–Batchelor were far more versatile than the sobriquet might imply.

Shorts: *Carnival in the Clothes Cupboard* (1941), *The Owl and the Pussycat* (1952), *The Figurehead* (1953), *Automania 2000* (1963), *The Butterfly Ball* (1974), *Autobahn* (1979), *Dilemma* (1981).

TV: *The Tales of Hoffnung* (1964, collected vt *The Hoffnung Symphony Orchestra*), *DoDo: The Kid from Outer Space* (1964), *The Jackson 5ive* (1971–3), *The Osmonds* (1972–4), *The Addams Family* (1973–5), *The Partridge Family: 2200AD* (1974–5).

Features: *Animal Farm* (1955), *Ruddigore* (1967; Batchelor alone).

Died (Halas): 1991
Died (Batchelor): 1995

WILLIAM HANNA & JOSEPH BARBERA

Born (Hanna): Melrose, New Mexico, 1910
Born (Barbera): New York, 1911
Notes: Two animators who reached their peak at MGM, creating a long sequence of brilliant Tom & Jerry cartoons, but who then

turned to TV, directing (later producing) endless series aimed largely at the Saturday-morning audience.

Shorts: *To Spring* (1936), *Puss Gets the Boot* (1940), *The Night Before Christmas* (1941), *Yankee Doodle Mouse* (1943), *Mouse Trouble* (1944), *Quiet Please* (1945), *The Cat Concerto* (1946), *Dr. Jekyll and Mr. Mouse* (1947), *The Little Orphan* (1948), *Hatch Up Your Troubles* (1949), *Jerry's Cousin* (1950), *The Two Mouseketeers* (1951), *Johann Mouse* (1952), *Life With Tom* (1953), *Touché, Pussy Cat* (1954), *Good Will to Men* (1955).

TV (much as producers rather than directors): *The Ruff and Reddy Show* (1957), *The Huckleberry Hound Show* (1958–62), *Quick Draw McGraw* (1959), *The Flintstones* (1960–66), *Top Cat* (1961–2), *The Yogi Bear Show* (1961–88), *The Jetsons* (1962–88), *The Adventures of Jonny Quest* (1964–5), *Shazzan!* (1967–9), *The New Adventures of Huck Finn* (1968–9), *Dastardly and Muttley and their Flying Machines* (1969), *The Perils of Penelope Pitstop* (1969–71), *Scooby-Doo, Where Are You!* (1969–72), *Wacky Races* (1968–70), *Hong Kong Phooey* (1974–5), *Jonny Quest* (1987), *The New Yogi Bear Show* (1988–9), *The Real Adventures of Jonny Quest* (1996–9), *What's New, Scooby Doo?* (2002–current).

Features: *Hey There It's Yogi Bear* (1964), *Alice in Wonderland, or What's a Nice Kid Like You Doing in a Place Like This* (1966), *Oliver and the Artful Dodger* (1972), *Charlotte's Web* (1973), *The Jetsons Meet the Flintstones* (1987), *Jetsons: The Movie* (1990).

Died (Hanna): 2001

HUGH HARMAN & RUDOLF ISING

Born (Harman): Pagosa Springs, Colorado, 1903
Born (Ising): Kansas City, Missouri, 1903
Notes: Two animators who were involved in the early days of Disney and who were formative in the creation of the Warners and MGM animation studios.

Shorts: *Sinkin' in the Bathtub* (1930), *Lady, Play Your Mandolin!* (1931), *One More Time* (1931), *Smile, Darn Ya, Smile* (1931), *Goopy Geer* (1932), *Shuffle Off to Buffalo* (1933), *Merbabies* (1938), *The Bear that Couldn't Sleep* (1939), *Jitterbug Follies* (1939), *Peace on Earth* (1939; Harman alone), *Wanted: No Master* (1939), *The Milky Way* (1940; Ising alone).

Died (Harman): 1982
Died (Ising): 1992

John Hubley

Born: Marinette, Wisconsin, 1914

Notes: One of the most innovative US animators, responsible for extending the application of limited animation and for opening the public's eyes to the appeal of experimental animation. Much of his later work was done in conjunction with his wife Faith (1924–2001), who was often uncredited.

Shorts: *Wolf Chases Pig* (1942), *The Dumbconscious Mind* (1942), *Professor Small and Mr Tall* (1943), *Brotherhood of Man* (1945), *Robin Hoodlum* (1948), *The Magic Fluke* (1949), *Ragtime Bear* (1949), *Spellbound Hound* (1950), *Gerald McBoing-Boing* (1951), *Rooty Toot Toot* (1952), *The Adventures of an * * (1957), *Moonbird* (1959), *The Hole* (1962), *The Hat* (1964), *Of Men and Demons* (1969), *Cockaboody* (1973), *Voyage to Next* (1974), *A Doonesbury Special* (1977).

Features: *Of Stars and Men* (1961), *Everybody Rides the Carousel* (1976), *The Cosmic Eye* (1985; Faith alone).

Died: 1977

Ub Iwerks

Born: Kansas City, Missouri, 1901, as Ubbe Ert Iwwerks

Notes: Created Mickey Mouse and many other characters for Disney, and made numerous technical innovations at that studio. Later set up on his own, with lesser success, then became a technical specialist for live-action movies, including Alfred Hitchcock's *The Birds* (1963).

Shorts: *Trolley Troubles* (1927), *Steamboat Willie* (1928), *The Skeleton Dance* (1929), *Fiddlesticks* (1930), *The Office Boy* (1932), *What a Life* (1932), *The Brave Tin Soldier* (1934), *Mary's Little Lamb* (1935), *The Air Race* (1936).

Died: 1971

Chuck Jones

Born: Spokane, Washington, 1912

Notes: One of the great Warners animators, who after the closure of that studio went on to others before making an important new career as an independent animator. The creator of several of the Warners series characters, including Pepe Le Pew, but known especially for Road Runner & Wile E. Coyote.

Shorts: *The Night Watchman* (1938), *Sniffles Takes a Trip* (1940), *The*

Dover Boys at Pimento University, or The Rivals of Roquefort Hall (1942), *My Favorite Duck* (1942), *The Aristo-Cat* (1943), *Odor-Able Kitty* (1945), *Duck Amuck* (1953), *One Froggy Evening* (1955), *What's Opera, Doc?* (1957), *The Dot and the Line* (1965), *How the Grinch Stole Christmas!* (1966), *The Cricket in Times Square* (1973).
TV: *The Bugs Bunny/Roadrunner Show* (1978–85), *The Bugs Bunny/Looney Tunes Comedy Hour* (1985), *The Chuck Jones Show* (2001–2002).
Feature: *The Phantom Tollbooth* (1969).
Died: 2002

WALTER LANTZ

Born: New Rochelle, New York State, 1900
Notes: Astonishingly productive animator with a lengthy career begun in his teens, best known as creator of Woody Woodpecker.
Shorts: *The Magic Lamp* (1924), *Boy Meets Dog* (1937), *Knock Knock* (1940), *Andy Panda's Pop* (1941), *Scrub Me Mama With a Boogie Beat* (1941), *Woody Woodpecker* (1941; vt *Cracked Nut*), *Chilly Willy* (1953), *Apple Andy* (1946), *Banquet Busters* (1948), *Private Eye Pooch* (1955).
TV: *The Woody Woodpecker Show* (1957–8, 1970–72, 1976–7), *Woody Woodpecker and Friends* (1958–66).
Died: 1994

JOHN LASSETER

Born: Hollywood, 1957
Notes: After stints at Disney and LucasFilm, co-founded Pixar, the CGI-animation studio that has become a commercially dominant force in animation on a global scale. He has also executive-produced the English-language versions of the Miyazaki movies *Spirited Away* (2002) and *Howl's Moving Castle* (2005), plus Pixar's *Monsters, Inc.* (2001), *Finding Nemo* (2003) and *The Incredibles* (2004).
Shorts: *Lady & the Lamp* (!979), *Luxo Jr.* (1986), *Red's Dream* (1987), *Tin Toy* (1988), *Knick Knack* (1989).
Features: *Toy Story* (1995), *A Bug's Life* (1998), *Toy Story 2* (1999), *Cars* (2006).

WINSOR MCCAY

Born: East *or* West Zorra, Ontario, Canada, 1867, *or* Spring Lake, Michigan, 1869 *or* 1871 (McCay gave varying accounts of his origins)
Notes: The most important single figure in animation history, with

the possible exception of Walt Disney; often called The Father of Animation, although he did not invent movie animation but rather launched it as a craze in the US – a craze that has never died.
Shorts: *Little Nemo* (1911), *How a Mosquito Operates* (1912), *Gertie the Dinosaur* (1914), *The Sinking of the Lusitania* (1918), *The Centaurs* (c1918–21), *Gertie on Tour* (c1918–21), *Flip's Circus* (c1918–21), *Bug Vaudeville* (c1921), *The Pet* (c1921), *The Flying House* (c1921; with Robert McCay).
Died: 1934

ROBERT MCKIMSON

Born: Denver, Colorado, 1910
Notes: One of the great Warners animators. Created the series characters Hippety Hopper, the Tasmanian Devil, Foghorn Leghorn and Speedy Gonzales. After Warners closed its animation studio he went with Friz Freleng to DePatie–Freleng.
Shorts: *Acrobatty Bunny* (1946), *Daffy Doodles* (1946), *Walky Talky Hawky* (1946), *Gorilla My Dreams* (1948), *Hop, Look and Listen* (1948), *Cat-Tails for Two* (1953), *Devil May Hare* (1954), *Tabasco Road* (1957), *Tortilla Flaps* (1958), *Bill of Hare* (1962), *Dr. Devil and Mr. Hare* (1964).
Died: 1977

NORMAN MCLAREN

Born: Stirling, Scotland, 1913
Notes: Doyen of experimental animators, a great nurturer of other animators, and stalwart of the National Film Board of Canada's world-acclaimed animation division. Made a Companion of the Order of Canada in 1973.
Shorts: *Love on the Wing* (1938), *Stars and Stripes* (1939), *Begone Dull Care* (1949), *Blinkety Blank* (1952), *Neighbours* (1952), *A Chairy Tale* (1957), *Mosaic* (1965), *Pas de Deux* (1968), *Ballet Adagio* (1971), *Narcissus* (1983).
Died: 1987

OTTO MESSMER

Born: West Hoboken, New Jersey, 1892
Notes: Creator (possibly with input from Pat Sullivan and/or John King) of Felix the Cat, for which Sullivan was given sole credit. An unsung hero of animation for over two decades after his retire-

ment until, in 1958, Joe Oriolo when reviving Felix for TV, made a point of according Messmer proper status.

Shorts: *Sammie Johnsin Hunter* (1916), *20,000 Laughs Under the Sea* (1917), *Feline Follies* (1919), *Felix in Fairyland* (1923).

Died: 1983

HAYAO MIYAZAKI

Born: Tokyo, 1941

Notes: "The Japanese Disney" – the most significant animator at work today and one of the two or three most significant animators of the past century. In the 1970s founded Studio Ghibli with colleague Isao Takahata, and from the 1980s has created a string of international hits.

Shorts: *On Your Mark* (1995).

TV: *Lupin III* (1971–2), *Great Detective Holmes* (1981; vt *Sherlock Hound*).

Features: *The Castle of Cagliostro* (1979), *Nausicaä of the Valley of the Wind* (1984), *Laputa: Castle in the Sky* (1986), *My Neighbor Totoro* (1988), *Kiki's Delivery Service* (1989), *Porco Rosso* (1992), *Princess Mononoke* (1997), *Spirited Away* (2002), *Howl's Moving Castle* (2005).

KATSUHIRO OTOMO

Born: Miyagi, Japan, 1954

Notes: Far more important as a creator of manga than as an animator, but nonetheless of importance to animation too, primarily as director of *Akira* (1987), based on his own manga and the first anime feature movie to make a real impact in the West. He also directed the live-action feature *World Apartment Horror* (1991).

Features: *Memories* (1996), *Akira* (1987), *Steamboy* (2004).

NICK PARK

Born: Preston, Lancashire, 1958

Notes: Astonishingly successful UK stop-motion animator who works at Aardman Animations, where he has created the characters Wallace & Gromit.

Shorts: *Creature Comforts* (1989), *A Grand Day Out* (1989), *The Wrong Trousers* (1993), *A Close Shave* (1995).

Features: *Chicken Run* (2000; with Peter Lord), *Wallace & Gromit: Curse of the Were-Rabbit* (2005; with Steve Box).

BILL PLYMPTON

Born: Portland, Oregon, 1946
Notes: Precocious independent animator who has blazed his own trail, producing often scurrilous movies distinguished by their savage wit.
Shorts: *Boomtown* (1985), *Drawing Lesson #2* (1987), *Your Face* (1987), *How to Kiss* (1989), *25 Ways to Quit Smoking* (1989), *Plymptoons* (1990), *Push Comes to Shove* (1992), *How to Make Love to a Woman* (1995), *Sex and Violence* (1997), *The Exciting Life of a Tree* (1999).
Features: *The Tune* (1992), *I Married a Strange Person!* (1997).

LOTTE REINIGER

Born: Berlin, 1899, as Charlotte Reiniger
Notes: Pioneering German animator who worked primarily with cut-paper silhouettes and who created the world's first animated feature movie.
Shorts: *Das Ornament des Verliebten Herzens* (1919), *The Stolen Heart* (1934), *Aucassin and Nicolette* (1975), *The Rose and the Ring* (1979).
TV: *Snow White and Rose Red* (1953), *The Three Wishes* (1953), *Sleeping Beauty* (1954), *Jack and the Beanstalk* (1955), *Helen La Belle* (1957), *The Seraglio* (1958).
Features: *The Adventures of Prince Achmed* (1926), *Dr. Dolittle and his Animals* (1928).
Died: 1981

RINTARO

Born: Tokyo, 1941, as Hayashi Shigeyuki
Notes: A Japanese master of TV animation who has more recently turned his full attention back to theatrical features.
TV: *Space Pirate Captain Harlock* (1978), *New Adventures of Kimba the White Lion* (1989), *Dragon Quest: Dai no Daibôken* (1991).
Features: *Astroboy* (1964), *Galaxy Express 999* (1979), *Dagger of Kamui* (1985), *Final Fantasy: Legend of the Crystals* (1994), *X* (1996), *Metropolis* (2001).

JAN ŠVANKMAJER

Born: Prague, 1934
Notes: Great Czech surrealist moviemaker who works usually in

a mixture of live action, puppetry and stop-motion animation, the latter generally done in clay. Almost by definition unlikely to have a movie showing at your local multiplex, but has made a certain commercial reputation through video/DVD releases in the West.

Shorts: *The Last Trick* (1964), *J.S. Bach: Fantasy in G-minor* (1965), *Punch & Judy* (1966, vt *The Coffin Factory*), *Historia Naturae (suita)* (1967), *Don Juan* (1970), *Jabberwocky* (1971), *Leonardo's Diary* (1972), *The Castle of Otranto* (1979), *The Fall of the House of Usher* (1980), *Dimensions of Dialogue* (1982), *Down to the Cellar* (1982), *The Pendulum, the Pit and Hope* (1983), *Darkness, Light, Darkness* (1989), *The Death of Stalinism in Bohemia* (1990), *Food* (1992).

Features: *Alice* (1988), *Faust* (1994), *Conspirators of Pleasure* (1996), *Otesánek* (2000; vt *Greedy Guts*), *Sílení* (2005; vt *Lunatics*).

ISAO TAKAHATA

Born: Ujiyamada, Japan, 1935

Notes: Co-founder with Hayao Miyazaki of Studio Ghibli in the 1970s, and a significant animator in his own right.

Shorts: *Panda & Child* (1972), *Panda & Child: Rainy Day Circus* (1973).

TV: *Lupin III* (1971-2), *Alpine Girl Heidi* (1974), *Three Thousand Miles in Search of Mother* (1976), *Anne of Green Gables* (1979).

Features: *The Little Norse Prince* (1968; vt *Horus, Prince of the Sun*), *Grave of the Fireflies* (1988), *Only Yesterday* (1991), *Pom Poko* (1994), *My Neighbors the Yamadas* (1999).

PAUL TERRY

Born: San Mateo, California, 1887

Notes: Founder in 1928 of Terrytoons, the studio that cranked out innumerable theatrical shorts for 20th Century–Fox, including cartoons featuring Mighty Mouse, Deputy Dawg, Heckle & Jeckle and Gandy Goose.

Shorts: *Little Herman* (1915), *Farmer Al Falfa's Wayward Pup* (1917), *Dinner Time* (1928), *Gandy the Goose* (1938), *The Mouse of Tomorrow* (1942), *Wolf! Wolf!* (1944), *Mighty Mouse and the Pirates* (1945), *The Talking Magpies* (1946).

Died: 1971

WILL VINTON

Born: McMinnville, Oregon, 1947

Notes: Before the advent of Aardman Animations, Vinton was the world's most significant creator of commercial stop-motion clay animation, using the process he trademarked as Claymation.

Shorts: *Closed Mondays* (1974), *Mountain Music* (1975), *Martin the Cobbler* (1976), *Rip Van Winkle* (1978), *Legacy: A (Very) Short History of Natural Resources* (1979), *The Little Prince* (1979), *The Diary of Adam and Eve* (1981), *James Weldon Johnson's The Creation* (1981), *Dinosaur* (1980), *A Christmas Gift* (1980), *Meet the Raisins* (1988), *The Raisins Sold Out!* (1990).

TV: *A Claymation Christmas Celebration* (1987), *Claymation Comedy of Horrors* (1991), *A Claymation Easter* (1992), *The Online Adventures of Ozzie the Elf* (1997), *The PJs* (1999-2000).

Features: *Little Prince and Friends* (1980), *The Adventures of Mark Twain* (1985), *Return to Oz* (1985).

RICHARD WILLIAMS

Born: Toronto, 1933

Notes: The "animator's animator" whose life has been dominated by the effort to complete the feature movie generally known as *The Thief and the Cobbler* (see page 47). Most famous for *Who Framed Roger Rabbit*. His earlier work for TV commercials raised the standards of TV animation to unprecedented heights.

Shorts: *The Little Island* (1958), *Love Me Love ME* (1962), *A Lecture on Man* (1962).

TV: *Charles Dickens' A Christmas Carol, Being a Ghost Story of Christmas* (1971), *Raggedy Ann and Andy: A Musical Adventure* (1977), *Ziggy's Gift* (1982).

Features: *Who Framed Roger Rabbit* (1988), *The Thief and the Cobbler* (1995; cut vt *Arabian Knight*, cut vt *The Princess and the Cobbler*).

"A little more to the west . . ."
Professor Calculus (*Hergé's Adventures of Tintin*)

TWO-DIMENSIONAL HEROES

Most commercial animated shorts have been released in one or other of the numerous series that various studios have created, and the cornerstone of the series has usually been a successful series character. These characters have come almost to possess the attributes of living people – of friends. Here are some of the more important ones.

1913

COLONEL HEEZA LIAR

Introduced by the Bray Studios in *Colonel Heeza Liar in Africa* (1913) and supposedly based on President Theodore Roosevelt, whose tales of courageous deeds were reputedly often enhanced. The diminutive adventurer, sometimes paired with his enormous wife, featured in nearly 60 shorts until *Colonel Heeza Liar's Romance* (1924).

MUTT AND JEFF

Born in Bud Fisher's newspaper strip, these two made it to the screen in *Mutt and Jeff* (1913), the first in a series of hundreds of shorts that ran until *The Globe Trotters* (1926). The shorts were churned out with such speed and under such tight budgets that, unsurprisingly, they're almost forgotten.

1916

FARMER AL FALFA

Paul Terry's great series creation, an elderly bearded farmer, appeared first in *Farmer Al Falfa's Catastrophe* (1916). Most of his other silent shorts appeared that year, as Terry had WWI army duties; a few came in 1920–23 after Terry's return. Later Terry revived the character for the talkies, beginning with *Club Sandwich* (1931); some 40 journeyman shorts followed until *The Dancing Bear* (1937).

THE KATZENJAMMER KIDS

This German-American family began life in 1897 as a comic strip, created by Rudolph Dirk, and entered the realm of animation with *The Captain Goes 'A-Swimming* (1916). There were about 35 silent shorts before production was cancelled in 1918 owing to WWI and the associated anti-German sentiment in the US. With similarly bad timing, they were brought back as Captain and the Kids in *Cleaning House* (1938), the first of a flurry of sound cartoons that ended with *Mama's New Hat* (1939).

KOKO THE CLOWN

His name later spelled Ko-Ko for copyright reasons, the clown was for a long while the Fleischers' premier series character, appearing first in *Out of the Inkwell* (1916) and then in scores of silent shorts until *Chemical Ko-Ko* (1929). He also appeared in a handful of the Fleischers' Talkartoons series from 1931.

KRAZY KAT

It was probably impossible to bring the surrealistic humour of George Herriman's comic strip to the cinema, but Krazy and Ignatz the Mouse first sparred onscreen in *Introducing Krazy Kat and Ignatz Mouse* (1916). Several score shorts followed, the series making the transition into sound smoothly with *Ratskin* (1929). The last was *The Mouse Exterminator* (1940).

1920

FELIX THE CAT

Created by Otto Messmer, this raunchy, ingenious little black cat was hugely popular during the 1920s and is still a recognizable icon today, appearing in countless cartoons (many earlier ones had no individual titles, so a count really is next to impossible) from *Feline Follies* (1920) to *Felix in the Last Life* (1928).

1925

PETE

Often known as Peg Leg Pete, the hulking bully who served so often as Mickey Mouse's nemesis in fact predates the Mouse, having appeared in 11 shorts prior to *Steamboat Willie* (1928). The first was *Alice Solves the Puzzle* (1925). Pete made over 40 shorts, and had roles in various Disney productions from the 1980s onward.

1927

OSWALD THE LUCKY RABBIT

The precursor to Mickey Mouse, and looking not dissimilar, appeared in 26 Disney silent shorts, beginning with *Trolley Troubles* (1927). The first Oswald cartoon to be made, *Poor Papa* (1928), was not released until quite late in the sequence; this was because Oswald's initial design – as a scruffy, fat, disreputable bunny – was rejected by the distributor. The last Oswald cartoon before Disney lost the copyright over a squabble with distributor Charles Mintz was *Sky Scrappers* (1928). Mintz thereafter commissioned Walter Lantz to recreate the character for sound cartoons, the new series beginning with *Ozzie of the Circus* (1929) and running for hundreds of shorts, mostly done by Lantz, until *Pixieland* (1938).

1928

MICKEY MOUSE

Walt Disney needed a new series character to replace Oswald the Lucky Rabbit, and so he dreamed up one whom he initially called Mortimer Mouse. Designed by Ub Iwerks and looking remarkably like Oswald, Mickey debuted in *Plane Crazy* (1928), though this was not his first short to be released: that was *Steamboat Willie* (1928), supposedly the world's first-ever sound cartoon. (In fact, there were a few precursors.) Mickey made about 120 appearances in theatrical shorts until the 1950s, then was revived in the 1980s. His television appearances are legion.

1930

BETTY BOOP

Animation's most enduring sex symbol first appeared as a dog in *Dizzy Dishes* (1930); this was a Bimbo cartoon, Bimbo the dog being a series star for the Fleischers. She gained her name in *Stopping the Show* (1932), and made over 100 cartoons thereafter. Her career was haunted by controversy: the Fleischers were sued by actress Helen Kane, upon whose appearance Betty's was partially based and of whose voice Betty's was a straightforward imitation; and there were constant protests about her suggestiveness. There's a touching moment in *Who Framed Roger Rabbit* (1988) when Betty encounters Jessica Rabbit and realizes sadly that, in terms of overt sexuality, she's living in a different era.

BOSKO

Warners' first series character and star of the first Loony Tunes cartoon, *Sinkin' in the Bathtub* (1930). Created by Rudolf Ising and Hugh Harman, Bosko was a little black boy designed to look not unlike Mickey Mouse; his various companions likewise had their counterparts in Disney's popular characters. He made a few score shorts for Warners before being taken by his creators to MGM for nine more, concluding with *Bosko in Bagdad* (1938).

FLIP THE FROG

Ub Iwerks's first series star after he'd left Disney to set up on his own, Flip debuted in *Fiddlesticks* (1930). This was in colour, predating Disney's first colour short, *Flowers and Trees* (1932), by two years. The earliest Flip cartoons show the frog as a more adult-appeal character; soon he was made cuter to rival other studios' creations. His farewell was *Soda Squirt* (1933).

PLUTO

Mickey Mouse's faithful hound Pluto first appeared unnamed in *The Chain Gang* (1930), was called Rover in *The Picnic* (1930), and finally became Pluto in *The Moose Hunt* (1931). In many of his 100 shorts he was support to Mickey or Donald.

1932

GOOFY

The bumbling loon of indeterminate species made his first appearance as a bit player in the Mickey Mouse short *Mickey's Revue* (1932), acquiring the name Goofy for *Orphan's Benefit* (1934) and clocking up over 80 shorts until the 1960s. Most popular were the "instructional" series of shorts, begun with the "How to Ride a Horse" section of the anthology feature movie *The Reluctant Dragon* (1941). The feature *A Goofy Movie* (1995) and its DTV sequel *An Extremely Goofy Movie* (2000) show a pale imitation of the original character.

1933

POPEYE

Originally called Ham Gravy, Popeye was born in 1919 in the comic strip *Thimble Theatre*, a creation of Elzie Segar; the name Popeye was introduced in 1929. Max Fleischer bought the screen rights, and the animated Popeye debuted in *Popeye the Sailor* (1933) as a support actor to  Betty Boop. Hundreds of Popeye shorts followed, the series concluding with *Spooky Swabs* (1957). Almost all featured Olive Oyl and the villain Bluto, with regulars like Wimp and Swee' Pea brought in later. The Robert Altman-directed live-action feature *Popeye* (1980), starring Robin Williams, flopped.

1934

DONALD DUCK

The irascible Duck made his first appearance as one of the ne'er-do-well farmyard animals in *The Wise Little Hen* (1934) and thereafter became perhaps Disney's most popular character of all, appearing in more shorts even than Mickey Mouse – about 160 in all – before sharing in the 1980s Disney revival of its classic characters.

1935

PORKY PIG

The stuttering pig who tells us "Th-th-that's All, Folks!" at the end of so many Warners cartoons made his debut in *I Haven't Got a Hat* (1935), a short that deliberately introduced a plethora of new characters (as schoolchildren) in an attempt to find a new series star. Few guessed it'd be the pig who'd find favour and go on to appear in over 150 shorts.

1937

DAFFY DUCK

Warners' duck, a more outwardly sophisticated character than Disney's Donald yet every bit as potentially rebarbative, was born in *Porky's Duck Hunt* (1937) and appeared in some 150 shorts thereafter. Like Bugs Bunny, he was a star of the live-action/animated movies *Space Jam* (1996) and *Looney Tunes Back in Action* (2003).

DAISY DUCK

As Mickey to Minnie, so Donald to Daisy, but in fact Daisy made very few appearances – astonishingly few, considering her popularity and reputation: a mere 12 until the 1950s, with some more after the general Disney revival of its classic characters from the 1980s onward. In her first appearance, *Don Donald* (1937), she was called Donna Duck; she became Daisy in her second short, *Mr. Duck Steps Out* (1940).

ELMER FUDD

Created by Tex Avery and born as Egghead (and looking quite unlike his later self) for *Egghead Rides Again* (1937), Elmer Fudd has been the nemesis manqué of Bugs Bunny or Daffy Duck – sometimes both – in well over 100 shorts; he gained the name Elmer J. Fudd in *Dangerous Dan McFoo* (1939), a Robert Service parody.

1938

BUGS BUNNY

Warners' trickster rabbit made his theoretical first appearance in Ben Hardaway's *Porky's Hare Hunt* (1938), although the first time he was really recognizable as Bugs was in Tex Avery's *A Wild Hare* (1940). Since then he's been in nearly 200 shorts and has been a mainstay of the live-action/animated movies *Space Jam* (1996) and *Looney Tunes Back in Action* (2003). The rabbit got his name because Hardaway's nickname was Bug; a rendering of the rabbit arrived for him at the studio labelled "Bug's Bunny" and the name stuck.

HUEY, DEWEY AND LOUIE

Donald Duck's three obnoxious nephews first arrived in the short *Donald's Nephews* (1938), and thereafter appeared in a couple of dozen shorts through the 1960s. The last, *Scrooge McDuck and Money* (1967), pointed the way forward: they became effectively Scrooge's nephews for numerous TV appearances and in particular in the Disney comics. They were Scrooge's costars in the feature movie *Duck Tales: The Movie – Treasure of the Lost Lamp* (1990).

1939

ANDY PANDA

Amiable cartoon panda initiated as a series star by Walter Lantz in *Life Begins with Andy Panda* (1939). Andy was extremely popular, but in his fourth short – *Knock Knock* (1940) – appeared the seed of his demise: one of the supporting cast was a lunatic woodpecker. There were over 25 Andy Panda shorts, but this number is dwarfed by the number Woody Woodpecker made.

1940

TOM & JERRY

Although William Hanna and Joseph Barbera will long be remembered for their countless animated TV series, their fame in the cinema rests largely on this pair of eternally feuding characters. No one else ever got Tom & Jerry right, not even Chuck Jones. In their debut, *Puss Gets the Boot* (1940), Tom belongs to an elderly black woman, Mammy, who cannot understand why he does so much damage while repeatedly failing to catch Jerry. Many of the hundreds of shorts that followed repeated this formula, but there were plenty where the animators allowed their imaginations to take wing, as in *The Cat Concerto* (1947), one of an astonishing total of seven Tom & Jerry cartoons to be recognized by an Oscar; indeed, between 1940 and 1954 Tom & Jerry had this roster of nominations:

> 1940: *Puss Gets the Boot*
> 1941: *The Night Before Christmas*
> 1943: *Yankee Doodle Mouse* (won)
> 1944: *Mouse Trouble* (won)
> 1945: *Quiet Please* (won)
> 1946: *The Cat Concerto* (won)
> 1947: *Dr. Jekyll and Mr. Mouse*
> 1948: *The Little Orphan* (won)
> 1949: *Hatch Up Your Troubles*
> 1950: *Jerry's Cousin*
> 1951: *The Two Mouseketeers* (won)
> 1952: *Johann Mouse* (won)
> 1954: *Touché, Pussy Cat*

The last Tom & Jerry short done by Hanna and Barbera was *Tot Watchers* (1958). A series done in 1961-2 by Gene Deitch made no impact, and likewise the 1963-7 series done by Chuck Jones and others. An animated feature attempting to capitalize on the characters' popularity was *Tom and Jerry: The Movie* (1992), dir Phil Roman; it flopped, but had DTV sequels.

WOODY WOODPECKER

Born as a support actor to Walter Lantz's series character Andy Panda in *Knock Knock* (1940), Woody stole that show and immediately became Lantz's most successful star, surviving in an uninterrupted series of hundreds of theatrical shorts until as late as 1972, with *Bye, Bye Blackboard*. For most of the run (from 1948 onwards; uncredited until 1952) Woody's voice was supplied by Grace Stafford, Lantz's wife.

1942

MIGHTY MOUSE

Called Supermouse for his first four shorts (they were later retitled), Mighty Mouse was a creation of I. Klein and Paul Terry and debuted in *The Mouse of Tomorrow* (1942). He appeared in over 60 shorts until *The Mysterious Package* (1961). On TV there was Terrytoons's *Mighty Mouse Playhouse* (1955–66), which at its peak eclipsed even Disney's *Mickey Mouse Club*. Filmation revived the character for the short-lived *The New Adventures of Mighty Mouse and Heckle and Jeckle* (1979–80). Later Ralph Bakshi created *Mighty Mouse: The New Adventures* in 1987; dogged by controversy about the sophistication of its content, this ran for just a couple of seasons but arguably represents US animated TV's finest hour.

TWEETY

The little airhead canary who somehow manages to evade capture by all cats was born in *A Tale of Two Kitties* (1942), a short supposedly starring two cats whom Warners thought might make successful series characters, Babbitt and Catstello (an attempt to rip off Abbott and Costello in animated form). Sometimes known as Tweety-Pie or Tweetie, the bird went on to make nearly 50 shorts, the vast majority of them with the cat Sylvester.

1943

CHIP AN' DALE

The two quarrelsome Disney chipmunks made their first appearance in *Private Pluto* (1943), were first named in *Chip an' Dale* (1947), and made a couple of dozen shorts. The TV series *Chip 'n Dale Rescue Rangers* premiered in 1989.

1945

CASPER

The creator of Casper, Joseph Oriolo, was paid an outright fee of $175 for *The Friendly Ghost* (1945), which everyone at the time assumed would be a one-off. However, the character was revived for *There's Good Boos Tonight* (1948), and scores of shorts followed until *Casper's Birthday Party* (1959). Then there were the TV career, the countless comics, the merchandizing ... culminating in the live-action/animated feature movie *Casper* (1995) with its DTV sequels *Casper: A Spirited Beginning* (1997), *Casper Meets Wendy* (1998) and *Casper's Haunted Christmas* (2000).

PEPE LE PEW

The amorous skunk with the atrocious French accent and the notoriously unsuccessful ways of charming the opposite sex – especially when they happen to be of the wrong species – appeared in about 16 shorts following *Odor-able Kitty* (1945).

SYLVESTER

Warners' cat, who aimed for shabby genteel but managed only the shabby part, made his debut in *Life With Feathers* (1945) and thereafter appeared in some 100 shorts. In about half of these he co-starred with the "innocent" canary Tweety; in a further dozen his co-star was Hippety Hopper, a childish-seeming kangaroo.

1946

FOGHORN LEGHORN

The jockish rooster made his initial appearance in *Walky Talky Hawky* (1946), supposedly a vehicle for Warners' relatively less successful series star Henery Hawk, and went on to make some 30 further shorts.

HECKLE & JECKLE

Created by Paul Terry, these two scheming magpies were identical except for their voices – one British, one American. They debuted in *The Talking Magpies* (1946) and made about 50 shorts until *Messed Up Movie Makers* (1966). Filmation revived the pair on TV for *The New Adventures of Mighty Mouse and Heckle and Jeckle* (1979–80).

1948

MARVIN MARTIAN

The lethal little robotic alien made his debut in *Haredevil Hare* (1948), which starred Bugs Bunny. Out of his half-dozen shorts, he is best known for his role opposite Daffy Duck in *Duck Dodgers in the 24½th Century* (1953).

YOSEMITE SAM

Always a supporting actor except in *Honey's Money* (1962), the small but mightily tempered cowboy debuted in *Buccaneer Bunny* (1948) and appeared in about 30 shorts before *Devil's Feud Cake* (1963). In almost all he was duelling wits with Bugs Bunny.

1949

MR. MAGOO

The brainchild of John Hubley, the crotchety near-blind plutocrat debuted in *Ragtime Bear* (1949) and appeared in over 50 shorts until *Terror Faces Magoo* (1959). Hubley did only the first three, most of the remainder being done by Pete Burness, including the series' two Oscar winners: *When Magoo Flew* (1955) and *Mr. Magoo's Puddle Jumper* (1956). In the 1960s a further flurry of Magoo cartoons came for TV. The live-action feature movie *Mr. Magoo* (1997), starring Leslie Nielsen, flopped.

ROADRUNNER & WILE E. COYOTE

The obsessive coyote – the hero of Acme Corporation's share-holders – and the target of his obsession, the bird seen usually as just a blur, were created by Chuck Jones for *Fast and Furry-ous* (1949) and continued what was essentially a single joke through some 40 shorts. Wile E. Coyote appeared in a handful of others sans Roadrunner, but in those he's basically a different character – a suave conman.

1951

GERALD MCBOING BOING

There were only five Gerald McBoing Boing shorts, beginning with *Gerald McBoing Boing* (1951) and ending with *Gerald McBoing Boing on the Planet Moo* (1956), but two won Oscars – the two just cited. The character, based on a Dr Seuss creation, was a small boy whose only words were "Boing Boing".

1953

SPEEDY GONZALES

The fastest mouse in the world first blazed across the screen in *Cat-Tails for Two* (1953), dir Robert McKimson; it is a common fallacy that his debut was *Speedy Gonzales* (1955), dir Friz Freleng, and that McKimson's version was just a rudimentary precursor. Speedy made over 40 shorts, almost all using the same basic repertoire of jokes.

1954

THE TASMANIAN DEVIL

Although he has become one of Warners' emblems thanks to his prolific TV career, this psychopathic creature has made only a half-dozen shorts, begun with *Devil May Hare* (1954).

1964

THE PINK PANTHER

Born in the credits animated by Friz Freleng for the live-action comedy-thriller *The Pink Panther* (1963), this character made his shorts debut in *The Pink Phink* (1964) and – often with his would-be nemesis L'Inspecteur – appeared in scores of shorts until *Supermarket Pink* (1980), with a late one-off, adapted from an episode of the successful Panther TV series, being released as support for the Don Bluth animated feature *The Pebble and the Penguin* (1995): *Driving Mr. Pink* (1995).

1989

WALLACE & GROMIT

The middle-aged kitchen-table inventor and his loyal dog, created by Nick Park, have featured in only three shorts (strictly speaking, featurettes) – *A Grand Day Out* (1989), *The Wrong Trousers* (1993) and *A Close Shave* (1995) – but the latter two won Oscars. The duo star also in the feature *Wallace and Gromit: Curse of the Were-Rabbit* (2005).

"I'm not in the book, you know!"
Gopher (Disney's *Winnie the Pooh* cartoons)

"Don't just stand there, do something!"
Dick Dastardly (*Dastardly and Muttley in their Flying Machines*)

Legendary Animations

Some animated movies are . . . well, *special*. For one reason or another, they have become the focus of constant discussion and even legend – just like *Casablanca* (1942) has become in live-action cinema. Here are some examples.

The Adventures of Prince Achmed
(*Di Abenteuer des Prinzen Achmed*)
dir Lotte Reiniger, 1926

Lotte Reiniger pioneered the art of silhouette animation; she painstakingly cut out her figures and background from paper. This art might not seem very important to the history of animation, but the earliest of Reiniger's animations possess even today a beauty and fascination that far transcend anything on offer from most animators of that era.

Paul Wegener, the actor and director probably best known for *Der Golem* (1915), in 1919 introduced Reiniger to a group who were setting up an experimental animation studio – Hans Cürlis, Berthold Bartosch and Carl Koch – with the suggestion that they should animate her silhouettes. She made her first silhouette movie with them, a short called *Das Ornament des Verliebten Herzens* ("The Ornament of the Lovestruck Heart"), in late 1919. Audience reaction was good, and she never looked back: all told she made over 50 shorts.

In 1923 she was approached by a banker, Louis Hagen, who offered to finance a feature-length movie of her silhouette animation; he also offered her a studio, specially built above his garage. Thus began the production of the world's first animated feature. With Bartosch, Koch (whom she had married in 1921) and Walther Ruttmann, she started work on *Die Abenteuer des Prinzen Achmed* (*The Adventures of Prince Achmed*; 1926), herself animating the action primarily with silhouettes and Ruttmann doing the backgrounds. The plot of the 90-minute movie is derived from several of the *1001 Nights* tales, and involves magic, romance and adventure.

It was filmed in black-and-white and then hand-tinted; in addition to the silhouettes there was animation using wax and sand, and there was some use of multiplane camera.

During the Allied bombing of Berlin in 1945, the negative and all known prints were destroyed. However, in 1954 a surviving black-and-white print was discovered in the archives of the British Film Institute. Later the colouring instructions that Reiniger had written back in 1925 were discovered, so the process of restoration could begin, being completed by 1970.

The movie was rapturously received in 1926. A second animated feature followed, in 1928: *Doktor Dolittle und seine Tiere* (*Dr Dolittle and his Animals*), based on Hugh Lofting's novel *The Story of Dr Dolittle* (1920) and with a score by Paul Dessau, Paul Hindemith and Kurt Weill. Unfortunately, the movie suffered the very considerable disadvantage that it wasn't a talkie – between the time Reiniger started work on it and its completion, sound movies had largely taken over from the silents.

A third animated feature would have followed based on Ravel's opera-ballet *L'Enfant et les Sortilèges* (*The Child and the Witcheries*; 1925), with libretto by Colette, but in the end – after some scenes had been animated and some sequences designed – getting the necessary copyright clearances from all concerned proved impossible.

⊞

Snow White and the Seven Dwarfs
dir David Hand, 1937

The first feature-length animated movie of the talkie era, and thus a landmark in the history of the cinema. It would certainly have bankrupted Disney had it flopped: at $1,480,000, an unprecedented sum in those days, it surpassed all the progressively larger budgets set for it, and was widely known before release as "Walt's Folly". Part of the cost involved new technical innovations (the movie cost about $200 per foot, compared with $50-$70 per foot for the

Disney shorts). All of this expense was incurred for a movie made when conventional Hollywood wisdom (the same wisdom that had doubted whether the fad for talking pictures would last) held that no audience would have the patience to sit through more than a few minutes of animation. Fortunately for Disney, both critical and popular reception exceeded all expectations, and the movie became one of the biggest commercial successes of all time . . . a success that continues to this day, with periodic re-releases of the movie in cinemas and on video/DVD.

A few objecting voices were raised at the time concerning the movie's scariness, which was thought to be too much for its supposedly juvenile audience. This objection seems to ignore two facts: first, fairy tales *were* often scary and gory, and many of them remained so even after the Victorian expurgations; second, children by and large adore gore.

More seriously, many both then and since have objected to the "Disnification" of the classic fairy tales, maintaining that the originals are, because of the popularity and commercial dominance of the Disney adaptations, becoming effectively lost to us. To this fear Walt Disney was insensitive, boasting that "in the end they'll probably remember the story the way we film it anyway".

Fantasia
1940

Although Disney had been matching music with animation from early on, with the *Silly Symphonies* series of shorts (begun in 1929 with *The Skeleton Dance*), the notion of an entire feature movie comprising such efforts was new. It seems to have sprung from a social encounter between Walt Disney and Leopold Stokowski, during which the conductor said he would like the two of them to work together on something. At the time the studio was working on a short based on Dukas's *The Sorcerer's Apprentice* (1897), and the whole project just growed and growed. The musical extracts were arranged by Stokowski, who also conducted the Philadelphia Orchestra for the performances.

The "The Sorcerer's Apprentice" section of *Fantasia*, with Mickey Mouse cast as the apprentice who disobeys sorcerer Yen Sid ("Disney" backwards) and uses a spell to make the broom bring in the water, is probably still today the movie's most famous, and the logo of Mickey dressed for the part has been a longstanding Disney emblem. Originally Dopey (from *Snow White and the Seven Dwarfs*) was proposed for the role.

Almost equally famous are the sections based on: Stravinsky's *The Rite of Spring* (1913), with lumbering dinosaurs; Moussorgsky's *Night on Bald Mountain* (c1866), with Chernabog (the Devil) waking from the hillside to receive the worship of assorted ghosts, ghouls, imps, etc.; and, for all the wrong reasons, Beethoven's 6th (*Pastoral*) Symphony (1808), which has capering centaurs, cutesy cupids and a rollicking Bacchus. On viewing the rushes of this latter segment, Walt Disney is widely reported to have said: "Gee, this'll make Beethoven."

The sequence directors were:
- ❋ James Algar: "The Sorcerer's Apprentice"
- ❋ Samuel Armstrong: "Toccata and Fugue in D Minor", "Nutcracker Suite"
- ❋ Ford Beebe, Jim Handley and Hamilton Luske: "Pastoral Symphony"
- ❋ Norm Ferguson and T. Hee (Walt Disney): "Dance of the Hours"
- ❋ Wilfred Jackson: "Night on Bald Mountain" and "Ave Maria"
- ❋ Bill Roberts and Paul Satterfield: "Rite of Spring"

Initially distributors RKO regarded *Fantasia* as, at two hours, impossibly long, and so an 81-minute version was prepared for general release – which release was not very successful. Even when offered financial inducement, only a few cinemas were prepared to install the expensive sound equipment (Fantasound) which Walt Disney insisted was necessary for enjoyment of the movie.

There were other bitternesses associated with the movie, not least over Stravinsky's horror at the unauthorized "improvements" Stokowski had made to his music.

During the 1960s a re-release of *Fantasia* brought the movie sudden popularity, its psychedelic surrealism appealing to hippy culture as the perfect accompaniment to the consumption of illegal substances – a cause of some embarrassment to the "family-friendly" Disney organization.

The movie was given a lacklustre "sequel" in 1999 in the form of *Fantasia 2000*. Of considerably more interest is Bruno Bozzetto's 1976 parody/homage *Allegro non Troppo* (see page 79).

Le Roi et l'Oiseaux
vt *The King and Mr. Bird*
dir Paul Grimault, 1980

French master-animator Paul Grimault directed the short *Le Petit Soldat*, based on a Hans Christian Andersen tale "The Brave Little Soldier", in 1947. Employed for the design on that short was his old friend Jacques Prévert, and immediately after it was finished they began working together on a feature, *La Bergère et le Ramoneur* (*The Shepherdess and the Chimneysweep*), again based on an Andersen story.

The years went by, and still *La Bergère et le Ramoneur* remained unfinished. Finally, with only three-quarters of the movie done and money seeming just to evaporate, André Sarrut, Grimault's partner in the production company Les Gémeaux, despaired, and in 1953 unilaterally released the movie as it by then was. Grimault and Prévert promptly disowned it. One or two distinguished names among the voice actors – e.g., Anouk Aimée as the shepherdess – and a soundtrack by the Royal Philharmonic Orchestra could not save the day. Widely anticipated to be the great breakthrough for French animation, *La Bergère et le Ramoneur* did only modestly on the home market and less well than that abroad.

The experience shattered Grimault, and for some 15 years he steered clear of animation except for a single educational short. In 1967, though, he managed to obtain the original negative of *La Bergère et le Ramoneur*, and realized he had the opportunity to finish it. The task involved not just completing the missing sections but also doing extensive redesign, modernization of the style, and story reconstruction, and it took him well over a decade. Finally, in 1980, the movie, now called *Le Roi et l'Oiseau*, was ready for release. The emphasis of the story had changed quite a bit, so the central figure was now a big black bird who befriended the lovers, rather than the lovers themselves.

The movie was at once acclaimed as the great French animation breakthrough that had been hoped for over a quarter of a century earlier. Of it Grimault remarked:"At the time we were making the film, we were in competition, cinematically, only with the Americans....They said animated cartoons were only for children or the parents who brought their children with them. Our aim was a bit different."

Little Nemo: Adventures in Slumberland
dir Masami Hata, William Hurtz, 1993

A movie based on Winsor McCay's longrunning comic strip from the early 20th century. King Morpheus of Slumberland sends Professor Genius to fetch the dreaming boy Nemo to be his heir, but *en route* Nemo stupidly lets the Land of Nightmare invade Slumberland, and Morpheus is abducted by the Nightmare King. Every now and then Nemo awakens in his bedroom and tells himself he has just been dreaming, only to witness dream reality re-invading his own.

The US/Japanese production was troubled. It had a high turnover of production staff, some being among the world's most distinguished animators, and was consequently years in the making. The credits line-up is astonishing: the screen concept was by Ray Bradbury; story consultants were David Hilberman, Oliver Johnston, Koji Shimizu, Frank Thomas and Robert Towne; the screenplay was by Chris Columbus, Fujioka, Moebius and Richard Outten; Moebius also did the conceptual design, with John Canemaker working on visual image development and Brian Froud on design development ... and so on.

The results were arguably worth the wait. The animation is wonderfully inventive and often spectacular, and there is the sense that all involved really *understand* the nature and appeal of fantasy: this is no superficial romp but is designed for repeated viewing to allow its various layers to be unpeeled. Bizarrely, in light of this, it received only a limited release, and there must be suspicions that the legendary Disney Dirty Tricks Dept. quashed what it saw as a major rival.

"You realize, of course, that this means war."
Bugs Bunny

The Thief and the Cobbler
dir Richard Williams, 1995

In about 1964 genius animator Richard Williams read some of the tales of Mulla Nasrudin, the wise fool of Sufi folktales. He contacted the London-based writer Idries Shah, and encouraged him to prepare a new edition of the tales which Williams illustrated; the result was the book *The Exploits of the Incomparable Mulla Nasrudin* (1966). This was the genesis of the animated feature the dream of which would impel his career for the next three decades.

Sometime in 1967–8 an early version of the soundtrack was recorded with Vincent Price (as the sorcerer ZigZag) and other actors including Sean Connery, Donald Pleasence and Anthony Quayle.

In 1969 the BBC produced a documentary about the project, which at the time had the provisional title of *The Golden City*. What emerged during this documentary was that Williams was reverting to full cel animation (animating 24 frames per second rather than the usual 12), and doing so by hand – there were no computer shortcuts being taken. The backgrounds Williams's studio was producing were dramatic in their lavishness and stylization, drawing upon both the Western and more importantly the Persian/Islamic tradition, with its strong emphasis on geometrical pattern and richness of colour.

Thanks to the BBC documentary, the project acquired considerable fame and prestige; but none of the major studios was prepared to put money into it. Income from animating television commercials, the stock-in-trade of Williams's studio, could go only so far. Against this background, in 1970 Williams accepted the commission to create a half-hour tv special version of Charles Dickens's novella *A Christmas Carol*. In accordance with a recurring motif of his career, he had difficulty finishing it on time and within budget, and in later stages Chuck Jones had to be called in to help (Jones is credited as Executive Producer).

The Dickens movie, screened in 1971, won an Oscar, and Paramount began negotiating a deal with Williams for the Nasrudin project. At first all seemed to be going well, but then Idries Shah's sister, who had done some if not all of the translations for the book

Williams had illustrated, claimed her copyright was being infringed. With the threat of litigation hanging in the air, Paramount nervously withdrew, leaving Williams to contemplate several years' worth of wasted animation. He was forced to trash all the work that had been done with the characters and situations that had appeared in the book and start all over again, salvaging what he could. He devised a new plot for what now came to be called *The Thief and the Cobbler*. (One of its later provisional titles was, ironically, *The Thief who Never Gave Up*.)

In about 1974 Williams was commissioned by 20th Century–Fox to act as animation supervisor on a feature movie to be based on Johnny Gruelle's nursery characters Raggedy Ann and Raggedy Andy. The revenue Williams received enabled him to resuscitate the Arabian project – this time only briefly, alas, because the poor take of *Raggedy Ann and Andy: A Musical Adventure* (1977) meant his money rapidly ran out.

In 1978, the Saudi Prince Mohammed Feisal stepped in with funding for Williams to make test footage for the revised project – a sequence called the Battle Scene. This was supposed to take only a few months but in the event took until the end of 1979, and cost over twice what Feisal had originally been quoted. Although the screening of the test sequence was received with a standing ovation, Feisal declined to fund the movie any further.

In 1984 Gary Kurtz – producer of *Star Wars* (1977) and many other movies – injected some money into the project and gave it some promotion to the studios; again there were no takers. However, Williams put together a 12-minute sample reel, and while in San Francisco arranged a screening for Milt Kahl, the venerable Disney animator. Stephen Spielberg, Robert Zemeckis and others involved in a planned feature movie based on Gary K. Wolf's novel *Who Censored Roger Rabbit?* (1981) heard about the reel, begged a screening of their own, and promptly commissioned Williams to be animation director of their own movie, eventually released as *Who Framed Roger Rabbit* (1988).

Thanks to the huge success of *Roger Rabbit*, Williams became the animator of the moment, and attention focused on the project about which there had been so much talk over the decades. Some funding came in from Japan, but most importantly Warners stepped in with a deal to complete the movie. Work went into high gear at Williams's London studio, with a planned release date that gradually receded into the future as time went on. In Spring 1992, Warners got wind of the upcoming Disney feature *Aladdin* (1992); little fancying their commercial chances in a head-on contest with Disney, Warners backed out of the deal.

But it seemed all was not lost. Budgetary overruns had been insured against with the Completion Bond Company, who could be expected to pick up the tab Warners had dropped. However, the Completion Bond Company itself was beginning to wonder if the movie would ever be completed. After discovering in June 1992 that there was still 15 minutes' worth of animation to be done, the company fired Williams and everyone else involved and hired TV animator/ producer Fred Calvert to finish the movie as cheaply as he could.

Calvert seems to have completed the project with as much integrity as possible given the stringent constraints placed upon him. For commercial reasons, some song sequences were added; these were largely done by Don Bluth's studio. Some sequences were eliminated from the original, for reasons unknown. In 1994 Calvert's version of the movie, for which no US distributor could be found, was released in Australia and South Africa as *The Princess and the Cobbler*. It did lukewarm box-office business.

In early 1995 Miramax, part of Disney, bought the movie for a song from the ailing Completion Bond Company, and hopes rose once more. But Miramax decided the existing version was still not commercial enough, and the entire project should be reworked. A new voicetrack was added, complete with the occasional anachronistic Disney-plugging pseudo-witticism. Much of the animation was cut, sequences of electrifyingly beautiful animation were rudely shouldered aside by Hollywood cliché, and the order of events was shuffled. The Miramax version, released in August 1995 as *Arabian Knight*, is a mess. As just one bizarreness, because Williams's original relied heavily on mime, with very little dialogue, much of the time the characters are speaking without moving their lips!

Williams retired from commercial animation after his movie had been taken from him by the Completion Bond Company. He is believed to be working on an animated movie of his own based on one of the plays of Aristophanes.

A LIBRARY OF JAPANIMATION

Japanese animation – known informally as Japanimation and more correctly as anime – was until recently a different world from mainstream Western animation. This situation was unchanged by the popularity in the West of Katsuhiro Otomo's *Akira* (1987), the first anime to make a significant impact on Western awareness. What really united the two schools of animation was the work of Hayao Miyazaki at Studio Ghibli. Movies like his *My Neighbor Totoro* (1988) succeeded in crossing all cultural boundaries, enabling him and others to present to appreciative Western audiences far more complex and quintessentially Japanese movies, such as his own *Spirited Away* (2002). (Miyazaki's animations are now so firmly a part of animation's mainstream that they're treated among the more general assembly later in this book: see page 75 onwards.)

At roughly the same time there was an explosion of lower-grade anime, presented for children, onto the TV screens of America. These series – which include *Pokémon*, *Sailor Moon* and others – became and still are enormously popular, fitting in with a juvenile culture that had already absorbed *Transformers*. Some of these series are by no means unremittingly bad – certainly a step up from the likes of *Scooby-Doo* – but they're outwith the scope of this book. Similarly outwith our scope are hentai – hard-core pornography anime, of which there are plenty.

Possibly the purest form of anime is to be found in the form of neither feature movies nor television but as DTV series, comprising 40- or 50-minute episodes, often a great many of them. This is the way anime is very often consumed in Japan, and the series have become popular in the West as well. Once more, these series, of which there are legion, are beyond the scope of this book. A good account of them is given in *The Anime Encyclopedia: A Guide to Japanese Animation Since 1917* (2001) by Jonathan Clements and Helen McCarthy. Here, in what is the briefest of tasters, we focus on feature movies.

Akira
dir Katsuhiro Otomo, 1987

Neo-Tokyo, 2019 (Tokyo itself having been destroyed in 1988 during WWIII), and a group of disreputable teenagers on the fringes of a repressive society must identify what precisely *is* the mysterious threat known as Akira, then try to neutralize it. Although the plot, based on a manga (graphic novel) series by Otomo, is very confused, the imagery and narrative are – just – sufficiently powerful to overcome such flaws.

Appleseed
dir Katsuyoshi Katayama, 1988

Based – like *Ghost in the Shell* (1995) – on manga by Masamune Shirow, this depicts a post-Holocaust Utopian society, Olympus, where genetically engineered people live in perfect harmony. Well, not quite perfect, because some seek to overthrow it. A member of a counterterrorist SWAT team seeks vengeance on the terrorist who killed her lover/partner, but slowly realizes the terrorist's aims might make more sense than she'd thought. The remake, *Appleseed* (2004), dir Shinji Aramaki, brings to bear an increased sophistication of animation – primarily CGI – but thereby loses whatever emotive qualities the original might have possessed.

Grave of the Fireflies
dir Isao Takahata, 1988

Exceptionally moving tale of two orphan children surviving in the aftermath of US saturation bombing late in WWII. It was because of this movie that the same studio's (Studio Ghibli's) *My Neighbor Totoro* (see page 82) could be made. There's a big market for educational movies in Japan. When the distributors showed doubts about *Totoro*, it was pointed out that it could make an excellent double bill with *Grave*, so the two were made alongside each other. The result? Two perennially popular masterpieces on the one double bill ...

Ninja Scroll
dir Yoshiaki Kawajiri, 1993

A classic of martial-arts anime. A ninja mercenary is caught up in a complex plot which involves him battling the Eight Devils of Kimon alongside a female ninja whose kiss, because her blood has been poisoned, is lethal.

Pom Poko
dir Isao Takahata, 1994

Urban sprawl threatens the wildlife on the edge of Tokyo, and the only ones that can resist it are the *tanuki* – intelligent semi-supernatural creatures that look like a cross between a badger and a raccoon, but with an enormous dangling scrotum. The *tanuki* are naturally best at fighting each other, but united under a matriarchal leader they battle in trickster fashion against the developers.

Ghost in the Shell
dir Mamoru Oshii, 1995

A cyborg officer in Tokyo's Section Nine security force in 2029 is concerned about the nature of her soul, if any; i.e., the ghost in her cyborg shell. She's leading the investigation against a criminal capable of hacking into not just machines but minds; it slowly dawns on her that he's looking for her as much as she's looking for him. What make this movie stand out, apart from the depth of its storytelling, are the beauty of its visuals.

The sequel was *Ghost in the Shell 2: Innocence* (2004).

X
dir Rintaro, 1996

With a plot that is well-nigh incomprehensible due to the need to explain vast tracts of the manga (written by the Clamp collective) on which it is based, this movie relies on some astonishing visuals; the animation itself is less impressive. Tokyo is threatened with destruction yet again – and, after Tokyo, the world – unless the ambiguous goodies succeed in a climactic battle involving gods and mortals.

Perfect Blue
dir Satoshi Kon, 1997

A very *noir*ish anime. A pop star decides to break into the movies as a second career, but is disturbed by some of the material she's expected to perform. Strange events multiply around her. How much of what we are seeing on the screen is really happening, how much her delusion?

Spriggan
dir Hirotsugu Kawasaki, 1998

The Japanese equivalent of *Raiders of the Lost Ark* (1981), the ark in question being this time Noah's Ark, located on Mount Ararat by a Japanese team whom it promptly blows to bits. Years later a young man ventures to Ararat in hopes of discovering the Ark's secrets, only to find a covert US Government team is after those same secrets with the aim of putting them to military use.

My Neighbors the Yamadas
dir Isao Takahata, 1999

Based on a successful comic strip, one of the most unusual anime features of all. Done in a diversity of artistic and animation styles, it presents a series of loosely linked – and wildly funny – episodes in the lives of a squabbling family.

Blood: The Last Vampire
dir Hiroyuki Kitakubo, 2000

A 1960s US Air Force base in Japan has become infested by shapeshifting vampires, and the only hope of the human inhabitants

– many of whom are themselves dressed as vampires, for this is Halloween – is a mysterious young swordswoman.

Cowboy Bebop: The Movie
dir Shinichiro Watanabe, 2001

Based on a successful TV series, this follows the adventures, in the distinctly Manhattan-like Alba City on Mars in 2071, of four bounty hunters who take on the task of catching the terrorist responsible for an explosion and find themselves in the middle of a far bigger and more horrifying plot that could threaten the entire city.

Metropolis
dir Rintaro, 2001

Having a loose basis in the classic Fritz Lang silent movie *Metropolis* (1927), this depicts a city divided much like the one in that movie, with robots occupying the lowest physical and social stratum. The robots are rebelling against oppression, while fascist elements of the human population are waging a clandestine dirty war against the robots. The tale is one of *noir*ish detection and doomed romance. The animation of the characters is somewhat rudimentary, but the rest is astonishingly fine.

Millennium Actress
dir Satoshi Kon, 2001

A moviemaker wants to make a documentary about the life of a retired screen goddess. As she tells him and his young assistant of her life and her cinematic career, past and present begin to blend into each other, as indeed does her biography with the screen roles she has played.

Tokyo Godfathers
dir Satoshi Kon, 2003

Derived from the old John Wayne movie *3 Godfathers* (1948), itself derived from various precursors, this sets in modern-day Tokyo a tale of three disparate homeless people who, despite themselves, on Christmas Eve take on responsibility for an abandoned baby they find, and strive against enormous odds to return it to its rightful parents.

Steamboy
dir Katsuhiro Otomo, 2004

There's a subgenre of science fiction known as steampunk, in which technological history (usually of the 19th century) is reimagined, with wonderful inventions appearing anachronistically. *Steamboy* is steampunk *par excellence*. It's the Industrial Revolution, and warmongering industrialists are fighting with each other over a marvelous new fuel which, if they have their way, will be used mainly to power bigger and better war machines.

*"M-M-Max Headroom
Heeeeeere!"*
Max Headroom

*"I knew I should have taken a
left turn at Albuquerque."*
Bugs Bunny

*"A baby's gotta do what a
baby's gotta do."*
Tommy Pickles (*Rugrats*)

"Eat my shorts"
Bart Simpson

SHORTS TO DIE FOR (NOT TO EAT)

Little Nemo
dir Winsor McCay, 1911

The first of McCay's groundbreaking cartoons and one of the first animated shorts ever made. In fact, the animation takes up only two minutes of the film's 10½-minute running time, the remainder being live action in which McCay bets friends he can complete 4000 animation drawings in a month, and then proceeds to do so. The animation is partly hand-coloured – i.e., with frames individually coloured on the film itself – and is based on characters from McCay's successful comic strip *Little Nemo in Slumberland*.

Gertie the Dinosaur
dir Winsor McCay, 1914

Again the animation, which required 10,000 individual drawings by McCay, occupies only part of this short, the remainder being live action in which McCay bets friends he can . . . A friendly dinosaur stomps around the primeval world performing various antics before, as climax, she takes a live-action McCay onto her back and walks off-screen with him. The short was designed to be part of McCay's highly successful roadshow, in which he gave theatrical performances of his astonishing drawing facility.

The Sinking of the Lusitania
dir Winsor McCay, 1918

McCay's most ambitious movie, again mixing live action with animation (25,000 drawings, and far more detailed than in his earlier
movies). The movie was a bellicose, partisan and factually dubious
call to arms in the wake of the sinking by German submarines of
the Cunard ship *Lusitania*. It played a part in the propaganda effort
to induce the US to enter World War I.

Feline Follies
dir Otto Messmer, 1919

The debut of Felix the Cat, here called Master Tom. Roué cat
Felix/Tom is crazy for Miss Kitty White. While they canoodle, the
mice in his house gleefully trash the place, and on return there he
is expelled by his owner as useless. He rushes to Kitty's, only to find
she has already birthed a litter of kittens that are quite obviously his.

KoKo's Earth Control
dir Dave Fleischer, 1927

Perhaps the best and most inventive of the Fleischer brothers' *Out
of the Inkwell* shorts, in which animation was mixed with live action
and the animator's hands could be seen as he drew the characters
into existence. KoKo and his dog discover the machinery that
controls the functioning of our world and start fiddling with the
levers – with surreally disastrous results.

Steamboat Willie
dir Walt Disney, Ub Iwerks, 1928

The third Mickey Mouse short and the first with sound; generally credited as the first animated talkie although in fact there had been a few earlier ones (e.g., Paul Terry's *Dinner Time*, just before). Mickey and Minnie cavort aboard a paddle-steamer, committing indignities upon farmyard animals.

The Skeleton Dance
dir Ub Iwerks, 1929

The first of Disney's long *Silly Symphonies* series. There's no real plot except that skeletons dance, although there's a vague correlation with the programme of Saint-Saëns' *Danse Macabre* – this despite the fact that the musical accompaniment is an adaptation of Grieg's *March of the Dwarfs*.

Three Little Pigs
dir Burt Gillett, 1933

Winner of an Academy Award™ and reviver of the fortunes of Technicolor, which company had been ailing. Three pigs build their houses according to the traditional nursery tale, and the Big Bad Wolf huffs and he puffs as he tries to blow the houses down. The song "Who's Afraid of the Big Bad Wolf?" was a massive hit and added a phrase to the language.

Poor Cinderella
dir Dave Fleischer, 1934

Betty Boop had first appeared in *Dizzy Dishes* (1930) as a cabaret singer with distinctly doggy features, supporting canine series character Bimbo. By the time of *Poor Cinderella*, her first colour outing, she had lost the dogginess and was the Fleischers' biggest star. Public outcry had already demanded Betty clean up her act a bit, but this very funny musical parody of the traditional tale is still packed with sexual symbolism.

"Heavens to Murgatroyd!"
Snagglepuss

Puss Gets the Boot
dir William Hanna, Joseph Barbera, 1940

The first Tom & Jerry cartoon, although Tom is here called Jasper. Tom/Jasper smashes an ornament while toying with Jerry, and his owner threatens that if he breaks one more thing he will be kicked out of the house. Thereafter Jerry does his best to break things so the cat will be blamed, while Tom/Jasper tries to stop him.

Superman
dir Dave Fleischer, 1941

The first of a series of 17 Superman shorts produced by the Fleischers in 1941-3, mostly dir Dave Fleischer, this was nominated for an Academy Award™. A Mad Scientist threatens humanity with his "electrothanasia ray", and Superman must save not just the world but Lois Lane.

Woody Woodpecker
(vt *Cracked Nut*)
dir Walter Lantz, 1941

The first Woody Woodpecker short, though not the first short in which Woody appeared: he was born as a supporting player to Andy Panda in *Knock Knock* (1940). In his debut as star, the other birds declare Woody to be "a nutcase"; his attempts to show otherwise only make him seem even nuttier.

The Dover Boys at Pimento University, or The Rivals of Roquefort Hall
dir Chuck Jones, 1942

A parody of snobbish college novels. The three Dover brothers share a fiancée, Dainty Dora Standpipe, and must rush to her rescue when she is abducted by dastardly Dan Backslide. The short is primarily of interest for its animation: Jones took the latest ideas in graphic design and added limited-animation techniques, demonstrating how use of the cheaper limited animation could be made a strength rather than a weakness. Alas, later animators mainly got the message that limited animation was cheaper.

Red Hot Riding Hood
dir Tex Avery, 1943

A cartoon that inflamed the puritanical fringe. It starts as a Disneyesque version of the traditional tale, but all three central characters – Red, Granny and the Wolf – protest to the director that they're tired of this "cissy stuff". He agrees, and the movie restarts with Red Hot Riding Hood as a nightclub singer, the Wolf as a lascivious fan, and Granny as a decrepit nymphomaniac. The short is homaged in the 1984 feature *The Mask*, where Jim Carrey, watching Cameron Diaz's nightclub act, reprises the Wolf's lecherous display.

Tweetie Pie
dir Friz Freleng, 1947

The first team-up between Tweety – his name misspelled in the title! – and Sylvester. A kindly human rescues Tweety from Sylvester's clutches and puts the bird in a gilded cage. The cat's cunning but doomed attempts to get his meal back are interspersed with beatings from his mistress. The short won an Academy Award™.

Cat-Tails for Two
dir Robert McKimson, 1953

Two dockland cats board a Mexican ship to catch mice, little realizing that one of those mice is "Senor 'Speedy' Gonzales, The Fastest Mouse in All Mexico". This first Speedy Gonzales short displays most of the speed gags that would be stock-in-trade for the successful series that followed.

Duck Amuck
dir Chuck Jones, 1953

Perhaps the most gleefully surreal commercial short ever made. Daffy Duck is put through a dazzling variety of personas and settings, the latter sometimes self-inconsistent, before at last the animator seems to hear his protests and brings on the "THE END" screen. But the argument and the short continue, at one point the ratchet slipping so two Daffies from adjacent frames can fight in a single frame. Finally the rogue animator is revealed to be Bugs Bunny.

Duck Dodgers in the 24½th Century
dir Chuck Jones, 1953

Bold adventurer Duck Dodgers (Daffy Duck) and eager space cadet Porky Pig (the brains of the partnership, believe it or not) are sent to Planet X to find the only remaining source of "aludium fosdex, the shaving-cream atom". There they find Marvin Martian, who asserts prior rights.

One Froggy Evening
dir Chuck Jones, 1955

A man discovers an all-singing-all-dancing frog and believes he can make his fortune from it. Alas, the fates conspire to ensure that, whatever fabulous performance the frog might put on, no one will ever witness it aside from the luckless owner.

Speedy Gonzales
dir Friz Freleng, 1955

Not the first Speedy Gonzales short, but the first to win an Academy Award™. A cheese factory on the US side of the US–Mexico border tantalizes Mexican mice, but they dare not cross over because of border guard Sylvester. The summons goes out for Speedy to save the day.

Birds Anonymous
dir Friz Freleng, 1957

Another Academy Award-winning short for Freleng and Warners. Sylvester is hauled by pious cat Sam into an organization akin to Alcoholics Anonymous but designed to help cats renounce their addiction to birds. Sylvester puts up a heroic struggle against his urges to devour Tweety, giving a whole new meaning to the phrase "cold turkey".

What's Opera, Doc?
dir Chuck Jones, 1957

A fairly standard Elmer Fudd and Bugs Bunny plot transported into Wagnerian opera, with Elmer as Siegfried and Bugs in various roles but most memorably as Brunhilde. Climactically, Elmer calls upon all the elements of nature to help him Smite the Wabbit, whom he then tragically mourns.

The Hole
dir John Hubley, 1962

Two labourers (voiced by Dizzy Gillespie and George Mathews) digging a hole under a New York street discuss the nature of accidents. One maintains the only way to stop the world being destroyed by accidental nuclear holocaust is to get rid of all nukes. The other mocks this as wimpish liberalism until a piece of heavy equipment accidentally falls, nearly killing them. This short won an Academy Award™.

The Pink Phink
dir Friz Freleng, 1964

The first of the Pink Panther shorts commissioned following the widespread acclaim for the animated credits Freleng created for the successful Blake Edwards/Peter Sellers feature *The Pink Panther* (1963). A homeowner decides to paint his house blue but of course that isn't the colour the Panther would prefer it to be . . .

How the Grinch Stole Christmas!
dir Chuck Jones, 1966

Based on the 1957 Dr. Seuss book, this tells of the mean old Grinch who tries to ruin Christmas for the occupants of a remote mountain village, only himself to be conquered by love.

Charles Dickens' *A Christmas Carol*, Being a Ghost Story of Christmas
dir Richard Williams, 1971

The plot of the 1843 Dickens tale boiled down to its essentials, but losing nothing of its emotional impact. This deservedly took an Academy Award™ for Williams.

The Cricket in Times Square
dir Chuck Jones, 1973

Based on *The Cricket in Times Square* (1960) by George Selden.

Connecticut cricket Chester C. Cricket is accidentally brought to Times Square subway station in Manhattan, where he befriends a newsstand boy. It emerges that Chester can make beautiful music with his wings, and his playing brings customers galore to the ailing newsstand.

The Small One
dir Don Bluth, 1978

In the Holy Land just before the birth of Christ, a boy takes an elderly donkey, Small One, to market to sell him. No one will buy except the butcher . . . and Joseph, who has hardly any money but needs a donkey – any donkey – to bear his pregnant wife Mary to Bethlehem for the census.

A Christmas Gift
dir Will Vinton, 1980

A homeless orphan and an old lady have the happiest Christmas of anyone in town over a candle, a crust of bread and a piece of cheese, which is all they have between them, because they discover sharing and true friendship.

Crac
dir Frédéric Back, 1981

A century ago, a Quebecois peasant chops down a tree and makes a wooden rocking chair for the woman he loves. The short is the story of the chair through all the decades until now, when it is the caretaker's chair in a modern art gallery – regarded by visiting children as the only true work of art in the place. *Crac* won an Academy Award™.

The Snowman
dir Dianne Jackson, 1982

Based on the 1978 graphic novel by Raymond Briggs. A young boy makes a snowman on Christmas Eve. That night the snowman comes to life and flies the boy to the North Pole, where he meets Father Christmas. Briggs's graphic novel about the latter character, *Father Christmas* (1973), was made into an animated short in 1991, dir Dave Unwin.

Vincent
dir Tim Burton, 1982

Done for Disney when Burton was working there. Seven-year-old Vincent Malloy wants to be like Vincent Price and infuriates his mother by staying in his room all day enacting horrors. The verse narrative is read by Price himself.

A Grand Day Out
dir Nick Park, 1989

The first Wallace & Gromit short, nominated for the Academy Award™ that was won by *Creature Comforts* (1989), also dir Park. Middle-aged, middle-class bachelor Wallace and his faithful, hyperintelligent dog Gromit discover they're out of cheese, and build a spaceship to go to the Moon in search of some. This was followed by two further Wallace & Gromit shorts, *The Wrong Trousers* (1993) and *A Close Shave* (1995), both of which won Academy Awards™.

The Death of Stalinism in Bohemia
dir Jan Švankmajer, 1990

Mixing animation with photomontage and archival footage, this offers a brief political history of Czechoslovakia after the Soviet occupation. What began as an attempted commission by the BBC evolved into a movie that is quite extraordinary in its pathos and power, even to those who do not recognize the personalities involved.

Geri's Game
dir Jan Pinkava, 1997

An old man playing solo chess imagines into existence a duplicate of himself as opponent, and the rivalry between the two intensifies. An Academy Award-winning short from Pixar.

"Kill the wabbit, kill the wabbit!"
Elmer Fudd (*What's Opera, Doc?*)

IN THE REAL WORLD: MIXING ANIMATION AND LIVE ACTION

The mixture of live action with animation is often thought of as a relatively recent phenomenon, one that had to wait until technology caught up with the idea. In fact, the notion predated that of all-animated movies.

A distinction must be made. Many, many modern live-action movies incorporate significant elements of special-effects animation, yet in no way can these sensibly be described as live-action/animated movies. The defining characteristic between the two forms is one of *intent*: special-effects animation intends to persuade the audience into accepting what is seen as real, while the animation in a live-action animated movie is foregrounded. Although *King Kong* (1933), *Godzilla* (1998) and *Scooby-Doo* (2002) all feature animated creatures operating in an otherwise live-action world, in the former two the purpose of the animation is – as with the character Gollum in Peter Jackson's *Lord of the Rings* movies (2001–03) – to create the illusion that the creature is real, whereas in the third the fact that the dog is an animated creation is an integral part of the movie's supposed appeal.

Out of the Inkwell
dir Dave Fleischer *et al.*, 1916–29

A very long series of shorts, latterly retitled *Inkwell Imps*. The trademark opening showed live-action hands drawing the figure of KoKo the Clown (later renamed Ko-Ko), who then sprang into animated life and thereafter often interacted with live-action humans. The first short in the series was *Out of the Inkwell* (1916), the last

Chemical Ko-Ko (1929), with further
Ko-Ko shorts thereafter being a
part of the Fleischers' *Talkartoons*
series.

The Alice Comedies
dir Walt Disney, 1923–7

Beginning with *Alice's Wonderland*
(1923, although not released until
some years later) and ending with
Alice in the Big League (1927), this series of 57 shorts featured a live-
action girl entering an animated world, where she had various
adventures with characters such as Julius the Cat and Peg Leg Pete.
The part of Alice was played by three different girls as the series
progressed: Virginia Davis, Dawn O'Day and Margie Gay. Walt
Disney, Ub Iwerks, Hugh Harman and Rudolf Ising were among
other human participants.

Song of the South
dir Harve Foster, anim dir Wilfred Jackson, 1946

Animated sequences based on exemplary tales from Joel Chandler
Harris's *Uncle Remus* (1880) and *Nights with Uncle Remus* (1883)
intersperse and illuminate a story of kids growing up in the old
American South. James Baskett was deservedly awarded an
honorary Oscar for his part as Uncle Remus, who tells the tales to
the kids, but this barely muted the accusations of racism aimed at
the movie, which seemed to glorify an era when everyone was
happy because "them darkies knew their place". That aside, the
animated sequences are charming.

Mary Poppins
dir Robert Stevenson, anim dir Hamilton S. Luske, 1964

Based on various novels in the children's series by P.L. Travers, this
was a smash hit for Disney and won Julie Andrews an Academy

Award™ as Best Actress. Two naughty kids seek the nanny of their dreams, and magical Mary Poppins (Andrews) sweeps into their lives to engage them in a series of fantasy adventures, one of which occurs in an animated world.

The Phantom Tollbooth
dir Chuck Jones, 1964

Based on the 1961 children's novel by Norton Juster, this follows the adventures of bored boy Milo, who in live action receives a vast gift-wrapped box from which spring a tollbooth and a car. He drives the car through the tollbooth, entering an animated world in which both he and the car are likewise animated. There he learns moral lessons from a variety of animated characters.

Bedknobs and Broomsticks
dir Robert Stevenson, anim dir Ward Kimball, 1971

Based on Mary Norton's children's novels *The Magic Bed-Knob* (1943) and *Bonfires and Broomsticks* (1947). During WWII, three kids evacuated from London are fostered by amateur witch Angela Lansbury. She empowers a bedknob with the magical ability to transport people to their destination of choice. In company with conman David Tomlinson they have various adventures, including one on an animated island where a wild soccer match is played.

Pete's Dragon
dir Don Chaffey, anim dir Don Bluth, 1977

Orphan Sean Marshall is sold into a vicious family, the only comfort the boy can turn to being his invisible friend, a huge (animated) dragon. After many adventures and with the dragon's assistance, the boy finds a new family and the dragon is proven to be real. There are clearly shades here of both *Harvey* (1950) and *Mary Poppins* (1964).

"D'oh!"
Homer Simpson

The Water Babies
dir Lionel Jeffries, anim dir Herbert Westbrook, 1978

Based on Charles Kingsley's 1863 novel *The Water-Babies*, this uses live action for all events occurring above water, animation for those beneath the water's surface.

TRON
dir Steven Lisberger, 1982

Rival cyberneticists are drawn into a vastly powerful computer whose megalomaniac Master Control Program views an experimental debugging program, TRON, as a threat. Live-action characters battle it out in an animated, video-game-like world. This cyberpunkish tale was probably ahead of its time.

Alice
vt *Neco z Alenky*
dir Jan Švankmajer, 1988

Based on Lewis Carroll's 1865 novel *Alice's Adventures in Wonderland* (1865). To say this is a faithful rendition would be reasonably accurate but highly misleading; the movie is a very surrealist interpretation of Carroll's tale, and thus not readily synopsized. Its power and effectiveness are, however, not to be questioned, and neither is its fidelity to the darker aspects of Carroll's inspiration.

Who Framed Roger Rabbit
dir Robert Zemeckis, anim dir Richard Williams, 1988

In 1947 Tinseltown, private eye Eddie Valiant (Bob Hoskins) is called in to investigate seeming adultery by Jessica Rabbit, wife of major Toon star Roger Rabbit. Although it proves Jessica is "not bad . . . just drawn that way", Eddie and Roger are drawn into a murderous conspiracy whereby Judge Doom (Christopher Lloyd) wishes to exterminate the entire population of Toontown, the ghetto next to Tinseltown where the Toons live. Based loosely on the novel *Who Censored Roger Rabbit?* (1981) by Gary K. Wolf.

Dick Tracy
dir Warren Beatty, 1990

A fairly typical Dick Tracy tale of corruption, gangsterism and a *femme fatale*, based on the comic strip created by Chester Gould, this places real actors in settings that are sometimes naturalistic but frequently animated. The effect of the partial animation is to imbue the flesh-and-blood cast with the illusion of toondom. Beatty himself is Tracy, Glenne Headley girlfriend Tess Trueheart, Madonna *femme fatale* Breathless Mahoney, and Al Pacino gangster boss Big Boy Caprice, while diverse stars have cameos.

Volere Volare
dir Guido Manuli, Maurizio Nichetti, 1991

Nichetti, whose job is dubbing Italian soundtracks for foreign animated movies, loves erotic-fantasy specialist Angela Finocchiaro but in her presence finds that more and more parts of his body develop toon attributes (and appearance). Once he becomes all toon, Finocchiaro, rather than rejecting him as ludicrous, realizes he is her ideal man – because in a way he does not exist – and falls blithely into his bed. Interesting here concerning the live action/animation interplay is that Nichetti's character is even in the flesh very toonlike: the message seems to be that we are more like toons than we'd prefer to believe.

Cool World
dir Ralph Bakshi, 1992

Comics artist and *crime-passionel* murderer Jack Deebs (Gabriel Byrne) is drawn into the Cool World, the realm he created in his comics, where he is seduced by nymphomaniacal nightclub singer Holli Would (played when in live action by Kim Basinger). She has plans for herself and all the Doodles of the Cool World to escape into ours.

> *"I'd've gotten away with it, too, if it weren't for you meddling kids . . . and your dog!"*
> various villains (*Scooby Doo*)

The Secret Adventures of Tom Thumb
dir Dave Borthwick, 1993

This surrealistic Bolex Brothers co-production, mixing live action with stop-motion animation, seems much influenced by the work of Jan Švankmajer. In an artificial-insemination plant, a fly falls into a flask, resulting in the birth of a tiny boy; developments thereafter are not easily synopsized. The live action is shot jerkily to give the illusion the actors are likewise stop-motion creations.

Faust
dir Jan Švankmajer, 1994

Loosely based on the libretto by Jules Barbier and Michel Carré for the opera *Faust* (1859) by Charles Gounod, and on many other Faust recountings, this mixes live action, puppetry and stop-motion animation as a modern-day actor falls into a highly fantasticated melange of Faustian events and images.

The Mask
dir Charles Russell, 1994

Repressed bank clerk and old-cartoons fan Jim Carrey falls for nightclub singer/gangster's moll Cameron Diaz. His love seems hopeless until he comes across an antique mask which, when he dons it, gives him supreme self-confidence and toon attributes. As The Mask he defeats organized crime and wins the lady. Based on the comics by Mike Richardson.

The Pagemaster
dir Joe Johnston, anim dir Maurice Hunt, 1994

In a vast library, a boy (Macaulay Culkin) accidentally knocks himself unconscious and is transported into an animated world where he is befriended by books as he makes his way through lands that are identified with fictional genres. The movie is not directly derived from but shares plot elements (and failings) with 1964's *The Phantom Tollbooth*.

Babe
dir Chris Noonan, 1995

Based on Dick King-Smith's children's novel *The Sheep-Pig* (1983; vt *Babe: The Gallant Pig*). Mixing live-action humans with animatronic animals, this charming movie tells of an orphaned pig, Babe, who seeks a career as a champion sheepdog – or sheep-pig. The sequel was *Babe: Pig in the City* (1998).

Casper
dir Brad Silberling, anim dir Eric Armstrong, Phil Nibbelink, 1995

The classic shorts character (see page 37) is resurrected for a feature. An evil heiress calls in ghost therapist Bill Pullman to unhaunt her haunted mansion, and boy-ghost Casper, taunted like the humans by his three nasty ghost-uncles, falls for the man's daughter, Christina Ricci. DTV sequels were *Casper: A Spirited Beginning* (1997), *Casper Meets Wendy* (1998) and *Casper's Haunted Christmas* (2000).

James and the Giant Peach
dir Henry Selick, 1996

Based on the 1961 children's novel by Roald Dahl, this has a live-action frame for an animated main adventure. Orphan James, at the mercy of two vile aunts, climbs inside a giant peach, and with the giant insects he meets there has adventures when the peach floats away.

Space Jam
dir Joe Pytka, 1996

Naughty aliens want to grab all the Looney Tunes characters for an amusement park. Bugs challenges them to a basketball game to decide matters. The aliens leech the talent of every basketball star they can find, but miss Michael Jordan, who's decided to try his hand at baseball. You can guess the rest.

The Adventures of Rocky and Bullwinkle
dir Des McAnuff, 2000

The "heroes" of Jay Ward's tv animated series are transformed into 3D CGI creations operating in the real world. Surrounded by a blizzard of all-star cameo parts, Boris and Natasha (Jason Alexander and Rene Russo) abet Fearless Leader (Robert De Niro) as he plans world domination through making US television stupider than it already is. Piper Perabo is FBI agent Karen Sympathy.

Cats and Dogs
dir Lawrence Guterman, 2001

Although we humans don't know it, the cold war between cats and dogs is being waged with all the high-tech sophistication deployed during our own Cold War. Live-action eccentric inventor Jeff Goldblum is trying to devise a canine allergy antidote, and of course the villainous cats will draw the line at nothing to stop him, up to and including murder!

Scooby-Doo
dir Raja Gosnell, 2002

The gang from the Hanna–Barbera tv series in a live-action adventure, with the title character rendered as a 3D CGI animation. The sequel was *Scooby-Doo 2: Monsters Unleashed* (2004).

Looney Tunes: Back in Action
dir Joe Dante, 2003

Daffy Duck is sacked by Warners executive Jenna Elfman and accident-prone security guard Brendan Fraser is told to escort him off the lot. Soon Daffy, Bugs and many other Looney Tunes characters are sucked into finding, before bad Steve Martin does, a jewel that could turn the planet's entire population into blue monkeys.

Spy Kids 3-D: Game Over
dir Robert Rodriguez, 2003

The third in a popular series. Juni (Daryl Sabara) and Carmen (Alexa Vega) are drawn into a desperate adventure inside an animated video game by a villain called The Toymaker (Sylvester Stallone). Within the game, the borderline between live action and animation is often blurred, and this teasing ambiguity is continued when some of the animations spill into the real world. The movie was initially released in 1950s-style 3D, complete with red/green goggles for the audience.

The Polar Express
dir Robert Zemeckis, 2004

Based on the 1985 children's book by Chris Van Allsburg, this performs the trick of converting live actors into animated characters; Tom Hanks plays several of the central parts. A boy who is agnostic about Santa's existence dreams up a train, the Polar Express, which takes him to the North Pole, where Santa utters appropriate homilies.

Sky Captain and the World of Tomorrow
dir Kerry Conran, 2004

Set in the future as envisaged from the 1930s and before, this uses live actors but alters their images so they appear to be CGI creations; they operate entirely in a CGI animated world. Aviator and general wrong-righter Sky Captain (Jude Law) and plucky Lois Lane-style reporter Polly Perkins (Gwyneth Paltrow) must thwart a villainous plot to destroy the world. The late Sir Laurence Olivier is digitally revived for a posthumous cameo role.

"Be quiet − be vewwy, vewwy quiet!"
Elmer Fudd

A LIBRARY OF
ANIMATED MOVIES

Gulliver's Travels
dir Dave Fleischer, 1939

Based loosely on the first part of Jonathan's Swift's 1726 novel, covering only the journey to Lilliput, this is the Fleischers' response to Disney's *Snow White and the Seven Dwarfs* (1937; see page 42). Gulliver, once reconciled with his Lilliputian captors, averts war between Lilliput and Blefuscu and solves the problem of a pair of crossed royal lovers.

Pinocchio
dir Ben Sharpsteen, Hamilton Luske, 1940

Based on the tale by Collodi (serialized from 1880 onwards), Disney's second animated feature displays some of the finest animation of all time. The wooden puppet who, given sentience by the Blue Fairy, wants to go further and become a Real Boy succumbs repeatedly to temptation despite the influence of his reified conscience, Jiminy Cricket.

Dumbo
dir Ben Sharpsteen, 1941

Despised by the rest of the circus animals because of his enormous ears, a baby elephant discovers he can fly. Short (63½ minutes) and uncomplicatedly animated, this is one of animation's most affecting features, and well merits its perennial popularity.

Hoppity Goes to Town
vt *Mr Bug Goes to Town*
dir Dave Fleischer, 1941

The Fleischers' second and final feature, and one of the neglected masterpieces of animation, this tells a complicated tale of love, treachery and politics within an insect community threatened by human property development.

Bambi
dir David D. Hand, 1942

Based on Felix Salten's 1929 novel, this celebrates the cycle of life through the tale of a young deer, Bambi, and his friends. The enemy most dreaded by all the forest animals is Man, who kills and destroys everything in his path.

Cinderella
dir Wilfred Jackson, Hamilton Luske, Clyde Geronimi, 1950

Based on the version of the tale given in *Histoires ou comtes du temps passé* (1697) by Charles Perrault, this is one of the most popular of Disney's retellings of classic fairy tales. The DTV sequel is *Cinderella II: Dreams Come True* (2002).

Peter Pan
dir Wilfred Jackson, Hamilton Luske, Clyde Geronimi, 1953

A surprisingly good amalgamation of the various versions J.M. Barrie produced of his great children's story, notably the play *Peter Pan*, first performed in 1904. The Disney animators did not always do well with children's classics by British authors, but in this instance the combination worked to produce what is still the definitive screen version of the tale. The sequel, *Return to Never Land* (2000), was far better than most such offerings.

Animal Farm
dir John Halas, Joy Batchelor, 1955

A reasonably faithful adaptation of George Orwell's 1945 novel, in which the farm animals throw out the drunken farmer and establish a republic . . . which eventually falls under the tyranny of the pigs. Widely regarded as anti-socialist or anti-communist, this is played more as a satire on human frailty and gullibility: unless we are watchful, our democracies will become tyrannies even while we are still hailing them as democracies.

Lady and the Tramp
dir Wilfred Jackson, Hamilton Luske, Clyde Geronimi, 1955
A new baby in a human family spells disruption in the pampered life of young spaniel Lady, and she flees to take up with ragamuffin mongrel Tramp. After many adventures, Lady is reunited with her loving owners, who also adopt Tramp. The DTV sequel is *Lady and the Tramp II: Scamp's Adventure* (2002).

Sleeping Beauty
dir Clyde Geronomi, 1959
Although coolly received on release, this is arguably the best of all Disney's adaptations of classic fairy tales; it is based, like 1950's *Cinderella*, on the version given by Charles Perrault. What the original critics disliked is what gives the movie its astonishing visual impact: the shift from realism to stylization in many of the background paintings.

One Hundred and One Dalmatians
dir Wolfgang Reitherman, Hamilton Luske, Clyde Geronimi, 1961
Based on Dodie Smith's children's novel *The Hundred and One Dalmatians* (1956), and using newly developed (by Ub Iwerks) animation techniques that both made the process cheaper and added an attractive stylized dynamism to the images, this tells of the quest by dogs Pongo and Perdita to save Dalmatian puppies from furrier Cruella De Vil. The DTV sequel is *101 Dalmatians II: Patch's London Adventure* (2003). The live-action remake was *101 Dalmatians* (1996), sequelled by *102 Dalmatians* (2000). The animated *101 Dalmatians: The Series* ran on TV 1997–8; associated were the TV movies *101 Days of 101 Dalmatians* (1995) and *101 Dalmatians: A Canine's Tale* (1996).

Gay Purr-ee
dir Abe Levitow, 1962
A screenplay that's surprisingly lacklustre bearing in mind that it's by Chuck and Dorothy Jones mars a movie full of visual excellence and some good songs. Parisian cat Mewsette (voiced by Judy Garland) is loved by rural unsophisticate Juane-Tom, but dastardly Meowrice has other plans for her.

The Jungle Book
dir Wolfgang Reitherman, 1967

Perhaps Disney's greatest travesty of a classic original, based on tales from Rudyard Kipling's *The Jungle Book* (1894). With devastating unsubtlety and raucous songs, the movie tells how Baloo the bear and Bagheera the panther save the orphan Mowgli from Kaa the snake and Shere Khan the tiger. Included here lest readers think it was omitted by oversight. The sequel is *The Jungle Book 2* (2003).

Yellow Submarine
dir George Dunning, 1968

The Blue Meanies have conquered Pepperland. Old Fred digs out the ancestral Yellow Submarine and flies with it to Liverpool to enlist the help of the Beatles in overthrowing the tyranny. Far better than it sounds, and with some stunning animation.

The Aristocats
dir Wolfgang Reitherman, 1970

A rich woman's will leaves her fortune to her cats; on their death it will pass to her butler. The butler naturally decides to speed the process up a bit, and tries to kill the cats, dumping their bodies far from home. But they survive, and have many adventures while returning to their loving owner.

Fritz the Cat
dir Ralph Bakshi, 1972

Based on the comics by Robert Crumb, this was an iconic movie of the hippy movement. The eponymous New York cat undergoes various escapades – some sexual, which caused a furore, and some drug-augmented – while thwarting neo-Nazi terrorists.

Charlotte's Web
dir Charles A. Nichols, Iwao Takamoto, 1973

Based on E.B. White's 1952 children's novel, this is Hanna–Barbera's artistically most successful animated feature, and has enjoyed long-standing popularity. A pig is being fattened for slaughter, but is befriended by the cunning spider Charlotte, who, through weaving words into her web, persuades humans the pig is possessed of miraculous intelligence and powers of prophecy.

La Planète Sauvage
dir René Laloux, 1973

Known to the English-speaking world as *Fantastic Planet* (vt *Planet of Incredible Creatures*, vt *The Savage Planet*), and based on Stefan Wul's 1957 novel *Oms en série*, this was one of those animated features a generation watched while smoking illicit substances. The human Oms live on a planet dominated by a (relatively) giant humanoid species, the Draags, who treat the Oms as vermin or, at best, pets. One pet Om turns rogue and leads his people to equality between the species. The movie's visuals have become near-iconic.

Allegro non Troppo
dir Bruno Bozzetto, 1976

In part a parody of/homage to Disney's *Fantasia* (1940), with adaptations of popular classics accompanying animated sequences, but thematically something much more, as the sequences cumulatively comprise an examination of human morality, warning of the perils of human vice. The key sequence, set to an extract from Stravinsky's *The Firebird*, shows the Serpent from Eden having an apocalyptic dream of humanity's technological future and likely demise.

The Rescuers
dir Wolfgang Reitherman, John Lounsbery, Art Stevens, 1977

Operating from a basement in the United Nations building in New York is the International Rescue Aid Society, a covert mouse organization dedicated to helping those in peril. Two contrasting mouse agents, proletarian Bernard and aristocratic Bianca, come to the aid of an orphan girl. In the excellent sequel, *The Rescuers Down Under* (1990), Bernard and Bianca travel to Australia to help a boy who's trying to protect threatened wildlife from poachers.

Wizards
dir Ralph Bakshi, 1977

A far-future fantasy in which good wizard Avatar must stop bad-wizard brother Blackwolf from conquering the world using a Nazi-like war machine. One of animation's most delightful and inventive fantasies.

The Castle of Cagliostro
dir Hayao Miyazaki, 1979

One in a series of movies, the rest by other directors, based on the manga by Monkey Punch, itself based (illicitly) on the Arsène Lupin stories by Maurice Leblanc. Romantic master-criminal Lupin III, a figure not unlike E.W. Hornung's Raffles, pursues a pretty girl and finds himself in the midst of a plot to destroy European economies, and worse.

The Fox and the Hound
dir Art Stevens, Ted Berman, Richard Rich, 1981
Based on the 1967 novel by Daniel P. Mannix, this tells of how a puppy and a foxcub become friends, despite universal disapproval.

Heavy Metal
dir Gerald Potterton, 1981
An anthology of short sections by different animation teams loosely knitted together by the EC Comics-style plot device of a glowing green ball which is supposedly the source of universal Evil. Some of the sections are entertaining, some less so; many feature underdressed babes. The movie is derived from and intended as a homage to the graphic magazine *Heavy Metal*, whose pages contain tales much like these. Much later came *Heavy Metal 2000* (2000), dir Michael Coldewey and Michel Lemire, a somewhat lifeless single-story confection whose working title was *Heavy Metal FAKK2*.

The Dark Crystal
dir Jim Henson, Frank Oz, 1982
Told in a mixture of puppetry, stop-motion animation and anything else Henson and Oz could throw in, this high-fantasy tale is enriched by a visual brilliance for which the artist Brian Froud was largely responsible. The elfin Gelflings are threatened by the vile Skeksis.

The Last Unicorn
dir Jules Bass, Arthur Rankin Jr, 1982
Based on the 1968 novel by Peter S. Beagle. Long ago the Red Bull drove all the unicorns to the edge of the world – all but one, Amalthea, who lacks both courage and character. With various lowborn friends, she quests to the castle of the Red Bull's master, Haggard, who tells her it was he who transformed the unicorns into breaking waves so he could have the sadistic pleasure of watching them strive for but never reach the land. Can Amalthea

summon the spirit to challenge the Red Bull and overturn the *status quo*? A remake is planned for 2006.

The Secret of NIMH
dir Don Bluth, 1982

Based on Robert O'Brien's 1971 children's novel *Mrs Frisby and the Rats of NIMH*, this tells how a widowed fieldmouse is helped to move herself and her children to safety by a community of super-intelligent laboratory-escapee rats which is itself in the midst of political upheaval. DTV sequels are *The Secret of NIMH 2: Timmy to the Rescue* (1998) and *The Secret of NIMH 3: Beginning* (2001).

Fire and Ice
dir Ralph Bakshi, 1983

A collaboration between Bakshi and Frank Frazetta, setting a fairly typical sword-and-sorcery adventure in what could be described as Frazetta's world – complete with muscular barbarian heroes and scantily clad babes.

Nausicaä of the Valley of the Wind
dir Hayao Miyazaki, 1984

Released in the West under various titles shuffling the words of the one above (the one to avoid is *Warriors of the Wind*, severely cut, and disowned by the director), this far-future fantasy epic pits a young girl who's simpatico with the creatures of a grievously polluted Earth against a warrior princess who seeks to restore the ecosystem by conquering it rather than cooperating with it.

The Adventures of Mark Twain
dir Will Vinton, 1985

Done in stop-motion animation, this shows Tom Sawyer, Huck Finn and Becky Thatcher stowing away on a balloon which Mark Twain flies to meet Halley's Comet – his destiny. *En route* Twain tells the kids some of his stories, shown as vignettes.

The Black Cauldron
dir Ted Berman, Richard Rich, 1985

Based on Lloyd Alexander's five *Chronicles of Prydain* novels (1964–8), this has been Disney's sole animated excursion into high fantasy, and was coolly received; later critics have been kinder. The pigboy Taran, with friends, must counter the plans of the Horned King to conquer the land.

An American Tail
dir Don Bluth, 1986

A family of Jewish mice escapes from antisemitic 1885 Russia to New York, where they are subject to the small mercies of corrupt officials and exploitative criminals – not to mention the city's ruthless cats. This has had three DTV sequels: *An American Tail: Fievel Goes West* (1991), *An American Tail III: The Treasure of Manhattan Island* (1998) and *An American Tail IV: The Mystery of the Night Monster* (1999).

The Great Mouse Detective
dir John Musker, Ron Clements, Dave Michener, Burny Mattinson, 1986

Based on Eve Titus's 1974 novel *Basil of Baker Street* (the movie has the vt *Basil – The Great Mouse Detective*), this posits a sleuthly mouse and his medico sidekick living beneath the apartment of Sherlock Holmes and Dr Watson. Like 1941's *Dumbo*, this modest movie demonstrated that in Disney animation modesty may be a virtue.

Laputa: Castle in the Sky
dir Hayao Miyazaki, 1986

Long ago, flying cities exerted military tyranny over the landbound. The father of orphan Pazu was derided for claiming to have seen the last of them, Laputa, still aloft. A young and very special girl, Sheeta, literally falls into Pazu's life. Aided by sky pirates, they must free Laputa before it is taken over and returned to evil uses by villain Mushka. Parts of the movie are based on Miyazaki's direct observation of the destruction of the Welsh coal industry and its associated communities by Margaret Thatcher. The vt *Castle in the Sky* is current in the US because people ignorant of Swift thought Hispanic parents might be offput by a title meaning "the whore" in Spanish.

The Land Before Time
dir Don Bluth, 1988

In the final days of the Age of Dinosaurs, five young herbivores have adventures on the long trek to the Great Valley, where food is legendarily plentiful. This has had numerous DTV sequels.

My Neighbor Totoro
dir Hayao Miyazaki, 1988

Two little girls whose mother is gravely ill find magic in the forest

near their new home. The "totoro" of the title is the mispronunci-
ation by the younger child of the Japanese word for "troll". A
completely captivating, charming masterpiece.

All Dogs Go to Heaven
dir Don Bluth, 1989

A murdered gangster dog goes to Heaven, because all dogs do,
whatever their behaviour in life. Despite being told Heaven is a
one-time-only offer, he returns to Earth seeking vengeance against
the gang boss who ordered his death . . . and in doing so discovers
all the doggy virtues of love and loyalty, so that an exception is
made and he can return to Heaven. This gave birth to a 1996–9 TV
series of the same name and had the DTV sequel *All Dogs Go to
Heaven 2* (1996).

Kiki's Delivery Service
dir Hayao Miyazaki, 1989

Trainee witches, to qualify as professionals, must spend a year living
alone and supporting themselves purely through their magical abil-
ities. One such is Kiki, and she finds it tougher than she bargained
for.

The Little Mermaid
dir John Musker, Ron Clements, 1989

Based exceptionally loosely on Hans Christian Andersen's 1837
tale. A young mermaid falls in love with a human prince and takes
to land to win him, despite the evil machinations of the sea-witch
Ursula. The DTV sequel is *The Little Mermaid II: Return to the Sea*
(2000).

DuckTales: The Movie – Treasure of the Lost Lamp
dir Bob Hathcock, 1990

Based on the longrunning comics series created by Carl Barks, this
was created by the Disney Movietoons unit and animated in
Europe. Scrooge McDuck and the three Nephews are up against
wicked sorcerer Merlock in a pulp-style Arabian adventure.

Beauty and the Beast
dir Gary Trousdale, Kirk Wise, 1991

Disney's return to classic fairy tales is a musical adventure featuring one of the studio's best-ever character creations, the Beast,
whose castle is populated by animated furniture and fittings. The

climactic scenes, as enraged villagers storm the castle, are a homage
to the old Frankenstein movies. Fine songs by Howard Ashman and
Alan Menken. The DTV sequels are *Beauty and the Beast: The
Enchanted Christmas* (1997) and *Belle's Magical World* (1998).

Aladdin
dir Ron Clements, John Musker, 1992

A so-so adaptation of the Arabian legend is saved by some stunning
animation. The DTV sequels are the fine *The Return of Jafar* (1994)
and the rather poor *Aladdin and the King of Thieves* (1996).

FernGully: The Last Rainforest
dir Bill Kroyer, 1992

From Australia, an ecological fantasy that competes with Disney on
Disney's terms, and arguably wins. The good witch of the rainforest,
who long ago imprisoned the local spirit of Evil in a tree, is dying,
and her young fairy heir, aided by a crackpot fruitbat, must guide the
ecosystem through the transition, protecting it from both the spirit
of Evil and the encroachment of human loggers. The DTV sequel is
FernGully 2: The Magical Rescue (1998).

Porco Rosso
dir Hayao Miyazaki, 1992

Some years ago an Adriatic pilot grew so tired of the world he
turned himself into a pig. Now it is the 1930s, and Italian fascism is
on the rise: Porco Rosso must resist the fascist forces, fight off
aerial pirates, thwart a hitman sent to get him, rekindle love, and
save the small aircraft business belonging to the family of an adoles-
cent friend.

The Tune
dir Bill Plympton, 1992

A tyrannical boss gives songwriter Del 47 minutes to come up with
a good song or be fired. Driving in panic to the office, Del takes a
wrong turn and arrives in the small town of Flooby Nooby, whose
local bizarres teach that songs are not to be written but to be
found. Plympton's inventive, often scatological, surreal zaniness at
full throttle.

The Nightmare Before Christmas
dir Henry Selick, 1993

Before he became internationally renowned as a live-action director, Tim Burton was a Disney animator, and he was the driving spirit behind his old employer's release of this stop-motion-animated feature (which has the vt *Tim Burton's The Nightmare Before Christmas*). In various mutually isolated townships live the characters associated with each of the major annual holidays. The story is set largely in Halloween Town, whose central figure, Jack Skellington, decides one year to usurp the role of Santa Claus and show how Christmas should *properly* be done.

The Lion King
dir Roger Allers, Rob Minkoff, 1994

Good songs (by Tim Rice and Elton John) and some awesome animation accompany the tale of young lion Simba having to fight off treachery in order to inherit his rightful place as King of the Pride Lands. The DTV sequels are *The Lion King II: Simba's Pride* (1998) and *The Lion King 1½* (2004; vt *The Lion King III: Hakuna Matata!*).

Toy Story
dir John Lasseter, 1995

The first Pixar animated feature, and a triumph. The toys in a boy's bedroom are thrown into consternation when his birthday brings a new arrival, the glitzy spaceman Buzz Lightyear, and none more so than Woody, the old-fashioned cowboy who until now has been undisputed Favourite Toy. Throw in a neighbouring boy who delights in performing abominations upon toys, and the stage is set for an excellent adventure. The masterful CGI animation was a revelation to the public; what tends to be overlooked is that the movie owes its success rather to excellent plotting, screenplay and characterization. The sequel, *Toy Story 2* (1999), is arguably even better.

Whisper of the Heart
dir Yoshifumi Kondo, 1995

Written by Hayao Miyazaki, this was directed by the protégé whom he planned would take over the helm at Studio Ghibli, so that Miyazaki himself might retire. Kondo's tragically premature death put an end to Miyazaki's retirement plans, and we're left with just the one movie from the man who might have been a new master. *Whisper* tells of highly intelligent but withdrawn schoolgirl Suzuku, who has romantic dreams and wishes to become a writer. She is led by a fat stray cat to a fascinating antique shop owned by an old man but seemingly ruled by the Baron, a distinguished cat statue who mysteriously possesses life. More immediately for Suzuku, the old man's grandson is her soulmate, a sensitive youth who yearns to be able to go to Cremona, Italy, where he might train as a violin-maker. A charming movie that is unjustly neglected.

Beavis and Butt-Head Do America
dir Mike Judge, 1996

Derived from the popular TV series, this sees the puerile pair hired by a gangster to go to Las Vegas and "do" his ex-wife. They accept with alacrity, assuming that "doing" the woman entails losing their long-resented virginities. In pursuit of her, they take in many of the US's significant sites, finding plenty of excuses for general smut at each of them.

The Hunchback of Notre Dame
dir Gary Trousdale, Kirk Wise, 1996

Loosely based on Victor Hugo's *Notre Dame de Paris* (1831). Monstrous bellringer Quasimodo falls in love with gypsy girl Esmeralda and saves her from the disgusting predations of vile hypocrite Judge Claude Frollo. It's difficult in animation to make a repulsively ugly hero sympathetic, but Disney managed the trick with seeming ease. The DTV sequel is *The Hunchback of Notre Dame II* (2002); five years elapsed between its completion and its release.

Anastasia
dir Don Bluth, 1997

A fantasy based on the legend that Princess Anastasia escaped when the rest of Russia's royal family were assassinated in 1918. The amnesiac orphan Anya slowly recovers her memory while, ironically, taking part in a scam that involves her pretending to be the long-lost Anastasia; meanwhile evil necromancer Rasputin does his best to kill her. The excellent DTV prequel *Bartok the Magnificent* (1999) merited the theatrical release it did not get.

Cats Don't Dance
dir Mark Dindal, 1997

A satire dressed up as a musical animated comedy for kids. The cat Danny arrives in Hollywood from Kokomo, Indiana, determined to be a Gene Kelly-style song-and-dance star, but runs straight into the psychological wall of prejudice: animals are suited only to bit parts, especially bit parts that stereotype their animalness.

Princess Mononoke
dir Hayao Miyazaki, 1997

Based on Japanese legend. An exiled youth must counter an aristocrat who, in her attempts to found and develop technological civilization, seeks to destroy the forest and the nature gods who dwell therein. In so doing he allies himself with wolf-reared wild girl San, the Princess Mononoke of the title (*mononoke* means "monster"). An epic work of animation.

Antz
dir Eric Darnell, Tim Johnson, 1998

Set in an anthill under authoritarian rule, *Antz* is a political satire dressed up as a talking-animals movie for kids. Woody Allen (in one of his best movie appearances in a while) voices the part of a Woody Allen-like ant who alone in the insect world has much by way of brains, yet finds intelligence on its own a weak weapon against militarism and totalitarianism.

A Bug's Life
dir John Lasseter, 1998

Pixar's second feature, released soon after the very similar *Antz* and overshadowing it. The anthill is threatened by martial grasshoppers, and young Flik sets off into the world to find allies to help resist the conquest.

The Prince of Egypt
dir Brenda Chapman, Steve Hickner, Simon Wells, 1998

Essentially, the life of Moses, dramatized and popularized so as to be suitable fare for a children's adventure. A solid animated feature from the Dreamworks studio.

The Iron Giant
dir Brad Bird, 1999

Based loosely on Ted Hughes's 1968 children's book *The Iron Giant*. A small boy befriends a giant alien robot that has crashlanded on Earth; between them they must save the planet from human warmongers in the teeth of opposition from the very people they're trying to save. This satire of the US's Cold War mentality is depressingly still relevant today, during the similarly paranoid "War on Terror".

South Park: Bigger, Longer, and Uncut
dir Trey Parker, 1999

Derived from the extremely popular adult TV series, and far more obscene than its original could be. The South Park kids inveigle their way into a cinema showing a scatological Canadian movie, and the next thing you know the US's right-wing Moral Minority has risen in fury and the US is declaring war on Canada. Saddam Hussein and Satan play their parts, too.

Tarzan
dir Chris Buck, Kevin Lima, 1999

Based loosely on Edgar Rice Burroughs's sequence of novels begun with *Tarzan of the Apes* (1914). The story is familiar; the movie is distinguished by a new animation process called Deep Canvas, which imbues the (beautifully rendered) backgrounds with an astonishing richness. The DTV sequels are *Tarzan & Jane* (2002) and *Tarzan II* (2005).

Chicken Run
dir Nick Park, Peter Lord, 2000

The first feature from the stop-motion studio Aardvark Animation: the traditional POW movie translated to a chicken run, where only the hen Ginger has the brains to try to avoid the otherwise inevitable future for the prisoners: becoming pies. Braggart circus performer Rocky arrives, a chicken cannonball flown off course, and with his uncertain support Ginger plans the Great Escape. Strong plotting and dialogue, constant inventiveness and superb characterization make this one of commercial animation's masterpieces.

Dinosaur
dir Eric Leighton, Ralph Zondag, 2000

Disney's first non-Pixar feature excursion into CGI is set in the days immediately preceding the cometary impact that brought about the extinction of the dinosaurs. An orphan baby dinosaur is reared by lemur-like mammals, and in turn saves them when the comet falls.

> *"Oh my God, they killed Kenny! You bastards!"*
> Stan and Kyle (*South Park*)

The Road to El Dorado
dir Eric Bergeron, Don Paul, 2000

No coincidence that the title echoes those of the Bing Crosby/Bob Hope movies of old, for this is a buddy comedy. Two crooks escape the brig of Cortes's ship and are worshipped as gods by the Mayan citizens of El Dorado.

Titan A.E.
dir Don Bluth, 2000

An animated excursion into space opera. Earth is destroyed by the alien Drej, and a small band of human survivors quests in search of the worldship/liferaft *Titan*, hidden somewhere among the starfields, which, once found, will unfold to become a fresh home for humanity, New Earth. Like its live-action precursor *Star Wars* (1977), this has a ramshackle plot but great action and visuals.

Final Fantasy: The Spirits Within
dir Hironobu Sakaguchi, 2001

Derived from a video game, this CGI science-fiction movie is remarkable for its astonishing realism and its frequent moments of considerable beauty. A young female scientist and her gruff mentor are intent on communicating with and preserving spirits whom most of the rest of the cast are unwittingly intent on destroying. The plot falls apart a bit in the final quarter, but by then the movie has done enough that this hardly matters.

Jimmy Neutron: Boy Genius
dir John A. Davis, 2001

Based on a TV series, this CGI movie, seemingly set in the 1960s, pits pre-adolescent genius inventor James Isaac Neutron and his pals against vastly superior invading alien forces. The plot moves like a rocket, every frame is packed with detail, and there are so many jokes that it doesn't matter if many of them misfire.

Monsters, Inc.
dir Pete Docter, 2001

Pixar's best fantasy to date, and perhaps the studio's best movie: an adventure based on the premise that it's the job of monsters based in an alternative world to terrify children in the nighttime bedrooms of our own world so that the energy of the kids' screaming can be used to power the other world's civilization. As usual with Pixar, great script, plotting, characterization and CGI animation.

Shrek
dir Andrew Adamson, Vicky Jenson, 2001

Based on the 1990 children's picture book by William Steig. The disgustingly ugly ogre Shrek merely wants to be left alone. A seedy local lord offers to ensure his solitude if Shrek will fetch him the lovely Princess Fiona to wed; needless to say, the ogre proves a better person than the lord. In the midst of the knockabout comedy there are numerous broad sideswipes at the prissiness of much traditional Disney animation. Sequelled by *Shrek 2* (2004), in which Princess Fiona, transformed into an ogress, must persuade her royal parents that Shrek is a suitable son-in-law.

The Cat Returns
dir Hiroyuki Morita, 2002

The Baron, the super-suave cat from 1995's *Whisper of the Heart*, features in another adventure. A girl saves the life of a cat that proves to be the prince of the Kingdom of the Cats. Transported there, she finds the ruthless king will have nothing but that she should marry the prince. Luckily the Baron intervenes.

Ice Age
dir Chris Wedge, 2002

It's the dawn of a new glacial period, and a human baby is left behind as his tribe flees the oncoming glaciers. A trio of unlikely companions comes to the rescue: a woolly mammoth, an irritating sidekick sloth, and a sabretooth cat who has other plans for the infant. Occasional laughs punctuate what's effectively a reprise of the 1948 Western *3 Godfathers* – another animated riff on which is 2003's *Tokyo Godfathers* (see page 55). Sequelled by *Ice Age 2: The Meltdown* (2006)

Lilo & Stitch
dir Dean DeBlois, Chris Sanders, 2002

Were it not for the quality of the animation, this slight movie might seem more a product of Saturday morning television, but it's so packed with energy and enthusiasm that it works. A fugitive alien criminal crashlands on Hawaii where he is innocently adopted by local girl Lilo, who thinks he's just an exceptionally ugly dog. Their friendship does wonders for both her dysfunctional family and his criminality. The DTV sequel is *Lilo & Stitch 2: Stitch Has a Glitch* (2005).

Spirited Away
dir Hayao Miyazaki, 2002

Conceptually Miyazaki's most complex fantasy to date. A whiny young girl, Chihiro, finds herself trapped in a strange and threatening edifice after her father takes a wrong turn on the road. Within the edifice, Chihiro enters a society made up of countless strange characters whose allegiances and personalities may remain forever impenetrable to her, but at least she succeeds in allowing her own personality to grow. This movie surprised many when, despite appallingly limited distribution, it carried off a well deserved Academy Award™.

Brother Bear
dir Aaron Blaise, Robert Walker, 2003

A young Inuit's brother is killed by a bear, and he follows the bear to kill it in revenge. Very soon, though, he is himself magically transformed into a bear, and the only way he can survive is by befriending other bears. He learns that all vengeance brings is destruction.

Finding Nemo
dir Andrew Stanton, 2003

The usual Pixar exquisite CGI, ultra-realism, beauty and superb feeling of space are brought to bear on this tale of a clownfish who loses his only child and scours the ocean in search of him.

Sinbad: Legend of the Seven Seas
dir Tim Johnson, Patrick Gilmore, 2003

The Goddess of Chaos is intent on creating discord among mortals, and at first glance the pirate Sinbad would seem an excellent choice as her unwitting agent. Yet the elaborate scheme she hatches involves the execution of a long-time friend of his, and she underestimates his sense of honour and basic decency.

Les Triplettes de Belleville
dir Sylvain Chomet, 2003

A surprising commercial hit (despite drastically limited release), and an unlikely Oscar nominee that had wide popular backing before being snubbed by the Academy. A cycling champion is abducted with others to the US, to Belleville (which is Manhattan under another name), to power a Heath Robinson-style machine controlled by a gangster boss. His grandmother doggedly tracks him down. Who can help free him and destroy the gangster? Who else but the eponymous singing 'n' dancing movie-star trio of yore, now three squabbling old ladies living in retirement. This is the animated movie Jacques Tati might have made with Quentin Blake, Ronald Searle and Gerald Scarfe as his concept artists.

The Incredibles
dir Brad Bird, 2004

Done in a starker style than Pixar's customary CGI lavishness. A family of superheroes forced into retirement by political correctness is lured back into the game. One of the best superhero movies of all, but marred by an Ayn Rand-style subtext praising social hierarchies and tacitly rebuking those who would seek to improve their lot.

Kaena: The Prophecy
dir Chris Delaporte, 2004

An anime-style CGI science-fiction movie from France/Canada. Freethinking girl Kaena lives amid a stagnating society in Axis, a giant tree upon whose fresh sap the community depends for sustenance . . . but the sap is running dry.

Shark Tale
dir Vicky Jenson, Bibo Bergeron, Rob Letterman, 2004

Piscine whale-wash (as in car-wash) employee Oscar gets the unwanted reputation of being a shark-slayer when one crashes into an anchor while trying to grab him. Meanwhile, the vegetarian son of the local shark mobster is causing his father angst. Enter a piscine *femme fatale* and . . .

Chicken Little
dir Mark Dindal, 2005

Chicken Little loses all credibility among the townsfolk when an acorn drops on his head and, in panic, he proclaims the sky is falling. Later, when the sky really *does* seem to be falling – an alien invasion is under way – he and his pals, knowing no one will believe them, must strive covertly to save the world.

Howl's Moving Castle
dir Hayao Miyazaki, 2005

Based on the 1986 novel by Diana Wynne Jones. Teenaged Sophie is transformed by a witch's curse into a nonagenarian, and as such becomes a cleaner in the household of the young wizard Howl, whose ambulatory castle is kept on the move through the powers of the fire demon Calcifer; as in the novel, its front door can open onto different worlds and times. The various stories of the plot are set against the backdrop of a futile war.

Robots
dir Chris Wedge, 2005

In a world reminiscent of 1950s America, the new manager of a robot factory wants to end the practice of making replacement parts for old models so that customers will be forced always to buy new. Naturally, our heroes thwart this scheme.

Tim Burton's Corpse Bride
dir Mike Johnson, Tim Burton, 2005

Burton's return to his great love, stop-motion animation, and also to the fascination with the dead that he displayed in 1993's *The Nightmare Before Christmas*. A shy bachelor escapes an arranged marriage at the last moment, and goes to live reclusively in the forest. There he attracts the amorous attention of the Corpse Bride, who guides him to the underworld.

Wallace & Gromit: The Curse of the Were-Rabbit
dir Nick Park, Steve Box, 2005

There's a big prize-vegetable show coming up, and the neighbourhood's produce is imperilled by rabbits. The much-loved screen duo are back, this time running a humane pest-control company. But Wallace is as always one invention ahead of the game: he could maybe build a machine that would stop rabbits wanting to devour plants . . .

"Mheep! Mheep!"
Road Runner

"That's all I can stands cause I can't stands no more!"
Popeye

AWARDS

ACADEMY AWARDS™

Note: The year is the year of release, not the year in which the award was given.

BEST ANIMATED FEATURE

This award has been given only since 2002, when the studios succeeded in their campaign to have proper recognition given by the Academy to animated movies; as an example of this near-complete neglect, we can note that even *Snow White and the Seven Dwarfs* (1937) failed to receive so much as a nomination, despite being quite clearly the outstanding feature-movie achievement of its year. The winners and nominees have been:

2001
Shrek, dir Andrew Adamson, Vicky Jenson
Jimmy Neutron: Boy Genius, dir John A. Davis
Monsters, Inc., dir Pete Docter

2002
Spirited Away, dir Hayao Miyazaki
Ice Age, dir Chris Wedge
Lilo & Stitch, dir Dean DeBlois, Chris Sanders
Spirit: Stallion of the Cimarron, dir Kelly Asbury, Lorna Cook
Treasure Planet, dir Ron Clements, John Musker

2003
Finding Nemo, dir Andrew Stanton
Brother Bear, dir Aaron Blaise, Robert Walker
The Triplets of Belleville, dir Sylvain Chomet

2004
The Incredibles, dir Brad Bird
Shark Tale, dir Vicky Jenson, Bibo Bergeron, Rob Letterman
Shrek 2, dir Andrew Adamson, Kelly Asbury, Conrad Vernon

BEST ANIMATED SHORT

Note: The precise title of this award has changed from time to time over the years.

1931–2 *Flowers and Trees*, dir Burt Gillett

1932–3 *Three Little Pigs*, dir Burt Gillett

1934 *The Tortoise and the Hare*, dir Wilfred Jackson

1935 *Three Orphan Kittens*, dir David Hand

1936 *The Country Cousin*, dir David Hand, Wilfred Jackson

1937 *The Old Mill*, dir Wilfred Jackson

1938 *Ferdinand the Bull*, dir Dick Rickard

1939 *The Ugly Duckling*, dir Jack Cutting

1940 *The Milky Way*, dir Rudolph Ising

1941 *Lend a Paw*, dir Clyde Geronimi

1942 *Der Fuehrer's Face*, dir Jack Kinney

1943 *Yankee Doodle Mouse*, dir Joseph Barbera, William Hanna

1944 *Mouse Trouble*, dir Joseph Barbera, William Hanna

1945 *Quiet Please!*, dir Joseph Barbera, William Hanna

1946 *The Cat Concerto*, dir Joseph Barbera, William Hanna

1947 *Tweetie Pie*, dir Friz Freleng

1948 *The Little Orphan*, dir Joseph Barbera, William Hanna

1949 *For Scent-imental Reasons*, dir Chuck Jones

1950 *Gerald McBoing Boing*, dir John Hubley

1951 *The Two Mouseketeers*, dir Joseph Barbera, William Hanna

1952 *Johann Mouse*, dir Joseph Barbera, William Hanna

1953 *Toot, Whistle, Plunk and Boom*, dir Ward Kimball, Charles A. Nichols

1954 *When Magoo Flew*, dir Pete Burness

1955 *Speedy Gonzales*, dir Friz Freleng

1956 *Mister Magoo's Puddle Jumper*, dir Pete Burness

1957 *Birds Anonymous*, dir Friz Freleng

1958 *Knighty Knight Bugs*, dir Friz Freleng

1959 *Moonbird*, dir John Hubley

1960 *Munro*, dir Gene Deitch

1961 *Surugat* (vt *Ersatz*, vt *The Substitute*), dir Dusan Vukotic

1962 *The Hole*, dir John Hubley, Faith Hubley

1963 *The Critic*, dir Ernest Pintoff

1964 *The Pink Phink*, dir David H. DePatie, Friz Freleng

1965 *The Dot and the Line*, dir Chuck Jones, Maurice Noble

1966 *Herb Alpert and the Tijuana Brass Double Feature*, dir John Hubley, Faith Hubley

1967 *The Box*, dir Fred Wolf

1968 *Winnie the Pooh and the Blustery Day*, dir Wolfgang Reitherman

1969 *It's Tough to Be a Bird*, dir Ward Kimball

1970 *Is It Always Right to Be Right?*, dir Lee Mishkin

1971 *The Crunch Bird*, dir Ted Petok

1972 *Charles Dickens' A Christmas Carol, Being a Ghost Story of Christmas*, dir Richard Williams

1973 *Frank Film*, dir Frank Mouris

1974 *Closed Mondays*, dir Will Vinton and Bob Gardiner

1975 *Great*, dir Bob Godfrey

1976 *Leisure*, dir Suzanne Baker

1977 *Sand Castle*, dir Co Hoedeman

1978 *Special Delivery*, dir Eunice Macauley and John Weldon

1979 *Every Child*, dir Derek Lamb

1980 *The Fly*, dir Ferenc Rofusz

1981 *Crac*, dir Frédéric Back

1982 *Tango*, dir Zbigniew Rybczynski[1]

1983 *Sundae in New York*, dir Burny Mattinson

1984 *Charade*, dir Jon Minnis

1985 *Anna & Bella*, dir Cilia Van Dijk

1986 *A Greek Tragedy*, dir Linda Van Tulden, Willem Thijsen

1987 *The Man Who Planted Trees*, dir Frédéric Back

1988 *Tin Toy*, dir John Lasseter

1989 *Balance*, dir Christoph Lauenstein, Wolfgang Lauenstein

1990 *Creature Comforts*, dir Nick Park

1991 *Manipulation*, dir Daniel Greaves

1992 *Mona Lisa Descending a Staircase*, dir Joan C. Gratz

1993 *The Wrong Trousers*, dir Nick Park

1994 *Bob's Birthday*, dir Alison Snowden, David Fine

1995 *A Close Shave*, dir Nick Park

1996 *Quest*, dir Tyron Montgomery, Thomas Stellmach

1997 *Geri's Game*, dir Jan Pinkava

1998 *Bunny*, dir Chris Wedge

1999 *The Old Man and the Sea*, dir Alexandr Petrov

2000 *Father and Daughter*, dir Michael Dudok de Wit

2001 *For the Birds*, dir Ralph Eggleston

2002 *The Chubb Chubbs!*, dir Jacquie Barnbrook, Eric Armstrong

2003 *Harvie Krumpet*, dir Adam Elliot

2004 *Ryan*, Chris Landreth

[1] Rybczynski went outside for a cigarette after receiving his award, was promptly arrested by those fun guys of the LAPD, and spent the night in jail

ANNIE AWARDS

The Annie Awards are organized by the Hollywood division of the International Animated Film Society – ASIFA-Hollywood. They originally celebrated lifetime technical/creative achievements, but in 1992 ASIFA introduced the category of Best Animated Feature.

1992 *Beauty and the Beast*, dir Gary Trousdale, Kirk Wise

1993 *Aladdin*, dir Ron Clements, John Musker

1994 *The Lion King*, dir Roger Allers, Rob Minkoff

1995 *Pocahontas*, dir Mike Gabriel, Eric Goldberg

1996 *Toy Story*, dir John Lasseter

1997 *Cats Don't Dance*, dir Mark Dindal

1998 *Mulan*, dir Tony Bancroft, Barry Cook

1999 *The Iron Giant*, dir Brad Bird

2000 *Toy Story 2*, dir John Lasseter

2001 *Shrek*, dir Andrew Adamson, Vicky Jenson

2002 *Spirited Away*, dir Hayao Miyazaki

2003 *Finding Nemo*, dir Andrew Stanton

2004 *The Incredibles*, dir Brad Bird

BIBLIOGRAPHY

Beck, Jerry (ed): *The 50 Greatest Cartoons, as Selected by 1,000 Animation Professionals*, Atlanta, Turner, 1994

Beck, Jerry, and Friedwald, Will: *Looney Tunes and Merrie Melodies: A Complete Illustrated Guide to the Warner Bros. Cartoons*, New York, Holt, 1989

Bendazzi, Giannalberto (trans Anna Taraboletti-Segre): *Cartoons: One Hundred Years of Cinema Animation* (revised edn), London, John Libbey, 2001

Clute, John, and Grant, John (eds): *The Encyclopedia of Fantasy*, London, Orbit, 1997

Frierson, Michael: *Clay Animation: American Highlights 1908 to the Present*, New York, Twayne, 1994

Grant, John: *Encyclopedia of Walt Disney's Animated Characters*, 3rd edn, New York, Hyperion, 1998

Grant, John: *Masters of Animation*, London, Batsford, 2001

Halas, John: *Masters of Animation*, Topsfield, Salem House, 1987

Holliss, Richard, and Sibley, Brian: *The Disney Studio Story*, London, Octopus, 1988

Lenburg, Jeff: *The Encyclopedia of Animated Cartoons*, 2nd edn, New York, Checkmark, 1999

McCarthy, Helen: *The Anime! Movie Guide*, London, Titan, 1996

Maltin, Leonard: *Of Mice and Magic: A History of American Animated Cartoons* (revised edn), New York, Plume, 1987

Patten, Fred: *Watching Anime, Reading Manga: 25 Years of Essays and Reviews*, Berkeley, CA, Stone Bridge Press, 2004

Peary, Danny, and Peary, Gerald (eds): *The American Animated Cartoon: A Critical Anthology*, New York, Dutton, 1980

Solomon, Charles: *Enchanted Drawings: The History of Animation* (revised edn), Avenel, NJ, Wings, 1994

Webb, Graham: *The Animated Film Encyclopedia: A Complete Guide to American Shorts, Features, and Sequences, 1900–1979*, Jefferson, NC, McFarland, 2000

Worley, Alec: *Empires of the Imagination: A Critical Survey of Fantasy Cinema from Georges Méliès to The Lord of the Rings*, Jefferson, NC, McFarland, 2006

Also of considerable usefulness are The Internet Movie Data Base (www.imdb.com), the *New York Times*'s online movie reviews archive (www.nytimes.com/ref/movies/reviews/index.html), and The Big Cartoon Database (www.bcdb.com).